# Free Speech

Other Books in the Current Controversies Series:

# Free Speech

**Scott Barbour**, *Book Editor*

**David Bender**, *Publisher*
**Bruno Leone**, *Executive Editor*

**Bonnie Szumski**, *Editorial Director*
**David M. Haugen**, *Managing Editor*

CURRENT CONTROVERSIES

Cover photo: © Clark Jones / Impact Visuals

Library of Congress Cataloging-in-Publication Data

Free speech / Scott Barbour, book editor.
        p. cm. — (Current controversies)
    Includes bibliographical references and index.
    ISBN 0-7377-0143-9 (lib. bdg. : alk. paper). — ISBN 0-7377-0142-0
(pbk. : alk. paper)
    1. Freedom of speech—United States. I. Barbour, Scott, 1963–      .
II. Series.
KF4772.Z9F737   2000
342.73'0853—dc21                                                    99-29107
                                                                        CIP

©2000 by Greenhaven Press, Inc., PO Box 289009, San Diego, CA 92198-9009
Printed in the U.S.A.

# Contents

## Chapter 1: Is Free Speech Threatened?

### Yes: Free Speech Is Threatened

## No: Free Speech Is Not Threatened

# Chapter 2: Should There Be Limits to Free Speech?

## Yes: There Are Limits to Free Speech

deems offensive from library collections, librarians are duty-bound to comply with the public's wishes. Librarians who oppose such decisions on the grounds that they are attempts at censorship are abusing their position.

## No: Free Speech Should Not Be Limited

# Chapter 3: Should Pornography Be Censored?

## Yes: Pornography Should Be Censored

explicit material is constitutionally protected speech. This conclusion is based on a distorted interpretation of the law. Americans must oppose the widespread acceptance of obscene words and images.

## No: Pornography Should Not Be Censored

place the decisions about Internet content in the hands of a small number of businesses.

# Chapter 4: Should Government Funding of the Arts Be Restricted?

# Foreword

By definition, controversies are "discussions of questions in which opposing opinions clash" (Webster's Twentieth Century Dictionary Unabridged). Few would deny that controversies are a pervasive part of the human condition and exist on virtually every level of human enterprise. Controversies transpire between individuals and among groups, within nations and between nations. Controversies supply the grist necessary for progress by providing challenges and challengers to the status quo. They also create atmospheres where strife and warfare can flourish. A world without controversies would be a peaceful world; but it also would be, by and large, static and prosaic.

## The Series' Purpose

The purpose of the Current Controversies series is to explore many of the social, political, and economic controversies dominating the national and international scenes today. Titles selected for inclusion in the series are highly focused and specific. For example, from the larger category of criminal justice, Current Controversies deals with specific topics such as police brutality, gun control, white collar crime, and others. The debates in Current Controversies also are presented in a useful, timeless fashion. Articles and book excerpts included in each title are selected if they contribute valuable, long-range ideas to the overall debate. And wherever possible, current information is enhanced with historical documents and other relevant materials. Thus, while individual titles are current in focus, every effort is made to ensure that they will not become quickly outdated. Books in the Current Controversies series will remain important resources for librarians, teachers, and students for many years.

In addition to keeping the titles focused and specific, great care is taken in the editorial format of each book in the series. Book introductions and chapter prefaces are offered to provide background material for readers. Chapters are organized around several key questions that are answered with diverse opinions representing all points on the political spectrum. Materials in each chapter include opinions in which authors clearly disagree as well as alternative opinions in which authors may agree on a broader issue but disagree on the possible solutions. In this way, the content of each volume in Current Controversies mirrors the mosaic of opinions encountered in society. Readers will quickly realize that there are many viable answers to these complex issues. By questioning each author's conclusions, students and casual readers can begin to develop the critical thinking skills so important to evaluating opinionated material.

Current Controversies is also ideal for controlled research. Each anthology in the series is composed of primary sources taken from a wide gamut of informational categories including periodicals, newspapers, books, United States and foreign government documents, and the publications of private and public organizations. Readers will find factual support for reports, debates, and research papers covering all areas of important issues. In addition, an annotated table of contents, an index, a book and periodical bibliography, and a list of organizations to contact are included in each book to expedite further research.

Perhaps more than ever before in history, people are confronted with diverse and contradictory information. During the Persian Gulf War, for example, the public was not only treated to minute-to-minute coverage of the war, it was also inundated with critiques of the coverage and countless analyses of the factors motivating U.S. involvement. Being able to sort through the plethora of opinions accompanying today's major issues, and to draw one's own conclusions, can be a complicated and frustrating struggle. It is the editors' hope that Current Controversies will help readers with this struggle.

Greenhaven Press anthologies primarily consist of previously published material taken from a variety of sources, including periodicals, books, scholarly journals, newspapers, government documents, and position papers from private and public organizations. These original sources are often edited for length and to ensure their accessibility for a young adult audience. The anthology editors also change the original titles of these works in order to clearly present the main thesis of each viewpoint and to explicitly indicate the opinion presented in the viewpoint. These alterations are made in consideration of both the reading and comprehension levels of a young adult audience. Every effort is made to ensure that Greenhaven Press accurately reflects the original intent of the authors included in this anthology.

*"A perpetual tension exists between free speech absolutists and those who favor restrictions on certain types of speech or expression."*

# Introduction

In the fall of 1997, students at Cornell University in New York stole 500 copies of the *Cornell Review*, a conservative campus newspaper, and burned them. The students were protesting the paper's inclusion of an editorial cartoon suggesting that African Americans have a disproportionate number of abortions. This incident followed a similar event the previous spring, when 200 copies of the *Review* were destroyed in response to the publication of a parody piece on Ebonics (Black English). These events—and a string of similar instances that have taken place on college campuses nationwide in recent years—illustrate that the ideal of free speech, so simple in theory, is often controversial in practice.

America's Founding Fathers believed so strongly in the right to free speech that they codified it in the First Amendment to the U.S. Constitution, which states in part, "Congress shall make no law . . . abridging the freedom of speech, or of the press." This right was considered so important it was the first of the ten freedoms protected by the Bill of Rights.

However, the right to free speech is not absolute. Throughout history, various restrictions have been imposed on this right by the Supreme Court. The classic examples of unprotected speech include fighting words and shouting "Fire!" in a crowded theater. Fighting words are those used to deliberately provoke a violent response from a particular person. Shouting "Fire!" in a crowded theater is outlawed due to its potential to endanger the public. These examples are often cited in attempts to determine whether controversial speech falls outside the scope of First Amendment protection.

Because the right to free speech is not absolute, a line must be drawn between acceptable and unacceptable forms of speech. Controversy arises when different parties disagree over where to draw that line. Indeed, a perpetual tension exists between free speech absolutists and those who favor restrictions on certain types of speech or expression, including hate speech, pornography, obscene art, sexually explicit library materials, and flag burning (which many people consider symbolic political speech). These and other forms of speech generate heated debate between those who demand completely unfettered expression and those who call for some degree of restriction on the words and images used by Americans.

The events at Cornell University reveal the complexity of the free speech debate. Many commentators harshly criticized the students who stole and destroyed copies of the *Cornell Review* simply because they found its contents distasteful. They also condemned the university's administrators, who did not intervene to stop or denounce the thefts. Critics insist that the right to free speech takes precedence over the sensibilities of the people who are offended by that speech. Furthermore, many contend that the most effective way to combat hateful speech is to respond to it rather than suppress it. In this way, it is believed, faulty reasoning, fallacies, and simple-minded bigotry can be exposed for what they are. As stated by Nat Hentoff, a columnist for the *Village Voice*, "The way to answer bad and hateful speech is with more speech—not with a match."

Others insist that certain forms of speech create harm by inflicting emotional pain or intentionally inciting others to violence. The speech that provoked the spring 1997 student protest at Cornell was considered more than merely offensive. The piece, written in Ebonics, parodied course descriptions from Cornell's Africana Studies and Resources Center. The description of the hypothetical course "Racism in American Society" included the following:

> Da white man be evil an he tryin to keep da brotherman down. We's got Sharpton an Farakhan, so who da white man now, white boy? . . . We ain't gots to axe da white man for nothin in dis class.

It is not difficult to understand why African-American students were outraged by this caricature of them. Nor is it hard to understand why using a match may have seemed a more appropriate response than simply the "more speech" recommended by Hentoff. As one Cornell student stated, "I'm tired of asking for my humanity."

The debate over the *Cornell Review* protests is mirrored in numerous contexts throughout American culture. Pornography and hate speech on the Internet, library books describing homosexuality as a lifestyle choice, violent and sexually graphic music lyrics—these are just a few of the other free speech issues on which Americans are sharply divided. All of these topics are the focus of *Free Speech: Current Controversies*. Throughout this anthology, authors debate where to draw the line between permissible and impermissible speech and expression.

# Chapter 1

# Is Free Speech Threatened?

# Chapter Preface

For many people, the American flag symbolizes all that is great about the United States, including the basic freedoms guaranteed in the Constitution and the Bill of Rights. But occasionally the flag becomes a symbol of protest— when it is burned or otherwise desecrated by persons opposing U.S. policies. In two separate decisions, in 1989 and 1990, the Supreme Court ruled that flag desecration is a constitutionally protected act of expression.

Many Americans disagree with this ruling and consider flag desecration an act of betrayal and an insult to veterans who have fought and died for their country. In 1995, and again in 1997, the House of Representatives passed a Constitutional amendment banning flag desecration; each time, the amendment failed to pass in the Senate. Patrick H. Brady, a retired major general and staunch supporter of a flag amendment, imagines how the nation's fallen veterans would respond to the knowledge that flag desecration remains legal:

> There is one issue which would hurt the most, which would turn them over in their graves, to see that it is legal to desecrate the Flag for which they fought. It is the only family portrait of all Americans, it is the sacred shroud which embraced their coffin, and which was the tissue for the tears of their loved ones.

Critics of the proposed amendment insist that such a ban would be a violation of one of the very freedoms the flag symbolizes: the freedom of expression. They agree with the Supreme Court that burning the flag is an act of protest worthy of constitutional protection. While most do not advocate flag desecration per se, they maintain that abolishing the right to do so would impinge on their liberties and open the door to further erosion of their rights. Lawrence Kolb, a Vietnam veteran who was assistant secretary of defense under Ronald Reagan, writes, "I revere the flag and that 'for which it stands.'" He nevertheless opposes the flag desecration amendment, stating, "The government may not prohibit the expression of an idea simply because society finds the idea offensive and disagreeable."

The debate over the flag desecration amendment is just one of the issues discussed in the following chapter. Other topics of discussion include freedom of the press, book banning, limits on political contributions, and speech codes on college campuses. In all of these cases, efforts to regulate the content of expressions are perceived as reasonable by some and as excessive intrusions by others.

# Censorship Threatens Freedom of the Press

**by Carl Jensen**

**About the author:** *Carl Jensen is a professor emeritus of communications studies at Sonoma State University and the founder of Project Censored, a media research project that attempts to identify issues that are systematically omitted by the U.S. mass media.*

Project Censored was founded in 1976 as a seminar in mass media at Sonoma State University in Rohnert Park, California.

The primary objective of Project Censored is to explore and publicize the extent of news censorship in our society by locating stories about significant issues of which the public should be aware, but is not, for a variety of reasons.

Since its inception, the Project has hoped to stimulate journalists to provide more news coverage of under-reported issues and to encourage the general public to demand more coverage of those issues by the media and to seek information from alternative sources.

The essential issue raised by the Project is the failure of the mass media to provide people with all the information they need to make informed decisions concerning their own lives. Only an informed electorate can achieve a fair and just society. The public has a right to know about issues that affect it and the press has a responsibility to keep the public well-informed about those issues.

## The Media Myth

We have all been brought up to believe in the power and value of the press—the great watchdog of society. It is the nation's ombudsman. It is the muckraking journalist with printer's ink in his blood who is willing to sacrifice all to expose evil. We were taught to believe *The New York Times* prints "All the news that's fit to print." We believed *The Chicago Times* when it said, "It is a newspaper's duty to print the news and raise hell."

I wanted to be a journalist from the time I was eight years old when I saw how important a newspaper, the *New York Daily News,* was to my father. He would bring it home each evening and sit at the kitchen table reading it from cover to cover before dinner. Later I came to believe that a journalist could make a difference and could even help to build a better world. . . .

The media-generated myth of the press as an aggressive, unbiased, honest watchdog of society, is just that—a myth. I fulfilled my child-hood dream of becoming a journalist but after witnessing first-hand the

> *"Only an informed electorate can achieve a fair and just society."*

kind of reporting it took to be a "successful" journalist, I left that profession for another which, at least, wasn't hypocritical about what it really was—public re-lations and advertising.

My early disenchantment with journalism only grew through the years as I first witnessed how advertisers could influence the media, and later, as a univer-sity professor, when I created a national research project—Project Censored—which explored and exposed the media's failure to cover important issues.

Admittedly, not all media and all journalists are driven by the bottom line but many are, especially the large media corporations and the "brand-name" jour-nalists. The media are more concerned with their next quarterly profit than with the unique opportunity given them by the First Amendment. And most journal-ists are more concerned with keeping their jobs and increasing their income than with fighting for the public's right to know. This helps explain why mil-lions of Americans turn to the alternative press for reliable information about what is really happening.

America's mainstream mass media basically serve three segments of society today—the wealthy, politicians, and the sports-minded. The news media have done an exceptional job of providing full and, on the whole, reliable informa-tion to those who are involved in or follow the stock market and to those who are involved in or follow politics and to those who are involved in or follow sports.

## Golden Age of Muckraking

At the same time, the media have failed to inform, or protect the interests, of those less fortunate in our society. It was not always this way. For a brief ten year period, at the turn of the century, a period sometimes referred to as the Golden Age of Muckraking, the media sought out, investigated, and published stories about the plight of all its citizens, including those at the bottom of the economic scale. The works of journalists and authors like Lincoln Steffens, Ida Tarbell, Upton Sinclair, and others, were widely read by many Americans and led to significant social change that benefited the general public.

Lincoln Steffens' *The Shame of the Cities* exposed and cleaned up municipal political corruption; Ida Tarbell's *The History of the Standard Oil Company* led to the dissolution of that giant monopoly; and Upton Sinclair's *The Jungle*, a powerful exposé of the meat packing industry, led to legislative changes and the first Pure Food and Drugs Act.

Sadly, nearly a century later, problems similar to these still exist. However, the muckrakers and the muckraking publications of yesteryear are not present today. Political bribes in government, earlier exposed by Steffens, are now often given in the acceptable form of PAC [political action committee] money and ignored by the press; the media not only fail to explain the negative impact of monopolies as Tarbell did, but instead act as cheerleaders for giant mergers; and instead of investigating and exposing the hazards and dangers of meat processing and packing as Sinclair did, the media are now content to sensationalize the deaths of children from e-coli rather than expose the conditions that create it. . . .

## News Censorship Is Not a Conspiracy

It is important to understand that the censored stories are not examples of some widespread media conspiracy to censor your news. News is too diverse, fast-breaking, and unpredictable to be controlled by some sinister conservative eastern establishment media cabal. However, there is a congruence of attitudes and interests on the part of the owners and managers of mass media organizations. That non-conspiracy conspiracy, when combined with a variety of other factors, leads to the systematic failure of the news media to fully inform the public. While it is not an overt form of censorship, such as the kind we observe in some other societies, it is nonetheless real and often equally as dangerous to the public's well-being.

Other factors accounting for censorship include the following: sometimes a source for a story isn't considered reliable (an official government representative or corporate executive is reliable; a freelance journalist or eyewitness citizen is not); other times the story doesn't have an easily identifiable "beginning, middle, and end" (acid rain just seems to go on for ever and ever); some stories are considered to be "too complex" for the general public (nobody would understand the intricacies of the savings and loan debacle); on occasion stories are ignored because they haven't been "blessed" by *The New York Times* or the *Washington Post* (reporters and editors at most of the more than 1500 daily newspapers in the United States know their news judgment isn't going to be challenged when they write

> *"The media-generated myth of the press as an aggressive, unbiased, honest watchdog of society, is just that—a myth."*

and publish fashionable "follow-the-leader" stories, a practice which leads to the "pack" or "herd" phenomenon in journalism).

Another excuse the media sometimes give is that the story is too old, outdated, or that they've already covered the issue. Just because a story was covered once doesn't mean the issue has been resolved. . . .

One major factor contributing to media self-censorship is that some stories are considered potentially libelous. Long and costly jury trials, settlements out of court, and occasional multimillion dollar judgments against the media, have produced a massive chilling effect on the press and replaced copy editors with copy attorneys. An equally ominous sign for freedom of the press was revealed in early 1997 when the Food Lion supermarket chain successfully sued ABC-TV after it aired an exposé of its meat packing procedures. Food Lion sued on the basis of a false job application, rather than libel, thereby circumventing libel laws designed to protect the press. Food Lion's argument was that the truth doesn't matter as much as the way the press goes after it.

However, the bottom line explanation for much of the self-censorship that occurs in America's mainstream media is the media's own bottom line. Corporate media executives perceive their primary, and often sole, responsibility to be the need to maximize profits for the next quarterly statement, not, as some would have it, to inform the public. Many [censored] stories do not support the financial interests of media publishers, owners, stockholders, or advertisers.

Investigative journalism also is more expensive than the "public stenography" form of journalism practiced at many media outlets. And, of course, there is always the "don't rock the boat" mentality which pervades corporate media boardrooms and then filters down to the newsroom. The latter influence has only been exacerbated by the number of megamedia mergers in recent history. The need to play it safe is becoming pervasive as the stakes are becoming increasingly higher.

## Censored Subjects

A statistical analysis of the top 200 stories over a 20-year period reveals that while there are some variations from year to year, and from election to election, on the whole, there has been a systematic omission of a select number of issues. The subjects most often censored since 1976 are political, corporate, international, and military issues.

Following are the number and percentage of all 200 censored stories by subject matter from 1976 to 1995:

| | | |
|---|---|---|
| 1—Political | 64 | 32.0% |
| 2—Corporate | 37 | 18.5% |
| 3—International | 30 | 15.0% |
| 4—Military | 28 | 14.0% |
| 5—Environmental | 15 | 7.5% |
| 6—Health | 13 | 6.5% |
| 7—Media | 7 | 3.5% |
| 8—Economic | 5 | 2.5% |
| 9—Education | 1 | .5% |

. . . The most disturbing result of this analysis is the number of issues that have still not been addressed by the major media since Project Censored first raised them.

Of the 200 censored issues, more than three quarters of them can still be classified as overlooked or censored by the mainstream media. Just 46 of the original stories have since received significant attention by the press. Some of the issues from the late 1970s that have been addressed include: acid rain, the fight over who controls the oceans' resources, freezing the elderly to death for non-payment of utility bills, and the commercialization of the Public Broadcasting System (PBS). Examples among the 150 issues that haven't been addressed include problems as near at hand as hazardous over-the-counter drugs and as far from home as the Indonesian repression in East Timor.

> *"America's mainstream mass media basically serve three segments of society today—the wealthy, politicians, and the sports-minded."*

By ignoring many critical issues in the past twenty years, the mainstream media have lost the confidence of the American people. Newspapers and network television news programs have lost many thousands—perhaps millions—of readers and viewers as recorded by circulation figures and television ratings. So many so that there is an industry term for the phenomenon: they call it "The Vanished."

However, it is still not too late to attempt to effect some change; we have an abiding faith in the will of the American people to want to know what is really happening in society, and, when so informed, to pressure politicians to do something about it.

## Slow to Respond

The 20-year span of time represented by the 200 stories in this analysis also reminds us of the length of time it takes us, as a society, to recognize and deal with these problems, if, indeed we ever do make the effort. Some examples include acid rain, a problem which we knew about in the early '70s but are only now starting to take seriously; the preventable deaths, injuries, and illness suffered in the workplace, which we knew about in 1976, but have yet to even acknowledge as a major national problem; the threat of male sterility caused by chemical pollution which first came to light in 1977 and yet even in the face of some startling research revelations about the worldwide drop in male sperm counts, it has yet to be put on the national agenda.

The single, most plausible, explanation for our failure to address these and other problems in a timely manner is found in our economic system. Capitalism dictates the need to make a profit—often regardless of the means necessary to achieve that profit. In the future, this era will be seen as one where we truly let significant problems get out of hand, a circumstance which led to the deterioration of much of our health and environment, a time when we permitted the robber barons to strip what was left of our earth's resources, a time when we allowed politicians to sell their souls to the highest bidder, and a time when we were distracted from the real issues of the day by media-hyped events such as the O.J. Simpson trial. It is a time when the few got wealthy at the expense of the many and Mother Earth was left to suffer. . . .

It is impossible to fully measure the impact the failure of the press has had on society. How many thousands, or perhaps millions, of lives would have been saved if the press had done its job instead of ignoring or covering up the problems? The lack of car safety features, the lax regulatory control of the airline industry, the link between tobacco and cancer, and the corporate greed of baby formula manufacturers that led to the deaths of thousands of Third World infants are just a few examples of where the media could have made a difference. How many millions of taxpayer dollars would have been saved if the media had exposed the savings and loan scandal in its infancy? And how much of our nation's resources could have been saved if the media had told the public about the scandalous Mining Act of 1872 that continues to give away valuable minerals and metals from federal lands for a song? . . .

## Junk Food News

Cynics say that the media give the public what it wants, i.e. "junk food news," because the people are not interested in reading about the issues raised by Project Censored. We contend that the public is not given the opportunity to read or hear those stories in the mainstream media and thus, unfortunately, will absorb only what the mass media offer. As author/poet T.S. Eliot warned presciently in 1923, "Those who say they give the public what it wants underestimate the public taste and end up debauching it." The inclusion of personality news, featuring people like Patty Hearst, Elvis Presley, John Lennon, Jim Bakker, Jeffrey Dahmer, O.J. Simpson, and Tonya Harding, among the top ten mainstream news stories in the United States, surely validates T.S. Eliot's warning.

The difference the press can make by doing the right thing is evident in the story of hunger in Africa. Hunger in Africa was consistently a "censored" subject during the early 1980s. When I would ask journalists why they did not cover the tragedy unfolding there, they would say, "It is not news," or, "Everyone already knows about starving Africans," or, "Nothing can be done about it anyway."

> *"One major factor contributing to media self-censorship is that some stories are considered potentially libelous."*

Early in 1984, an ABC-TV News correspondent in Rome came upon information that led him to believe that millions of lives were being threatened by drought and famine in Africa. He asked the ABC home office in New York for permission to take his crew to Africa to get the story. The answer was no.

Later, a BBC television crew, traveling through Ethiopia, captured the horrifying reality of children starving to death. When the world saw the bloated stomachs and bony limbs of the starving children on their television sets, it sparked a worldwide reaction, including an internationally televised rock-fest called Live Aid and the musical anthem, "We Are The World," that reportedly saved the lives of seven million Ethiopians.

Indeed the media can make a difference.

## We Must Support a Free Press

It is the media's responsibility, as true watchdogs of society with the unique protection of the First Amendment, to explore, compile, and present information that people should be aware of in a way that will attract their attention and be relevant to their everyday lives. And, when the media do this, people will read and respond to the issues raised. And journalists need not be embarrassed when they cash their paychecks.

The press does have the power to stimulate people to clean up the environment; to prevent nuclear proliferation; to force corrupt politicians out of office; to reduce poverty; to provide quality health care for all people; to create a truly equitable, fair, and just society. . . . This is why we must all look to, prod, and support a free, open, and aggressive press. We have a free press in the United States guaranteed by the First Amendment and we have the best communications technology in world history. Now let us seek a more responsible and responsive press—a press that earns its First Amendment rights the old-fashioned way. Indeed, a press not afraid to do a little muckraking. Then, and only then, will we have the information we need to build a more enlightened and responsive society.

# Book Banning Threatens Free Speech

**by American Civil Liberties Union**

**About the author:** *The American Civil Liberties Union (ACLU) is a national organization dedicated to protecting Americans' constitutional liberties.*

> *"I'm completely appalled at the excerpts. I feel that this is a degradation of the human race."*
>
> —September 1998 statement by Prince William School Board member John Harper Jr., discussing parents' complaints about the books *Nightjohn, Go Tell It on the Mountain,* and *Slaughterhouse Five* on school summer reading lists.

Banned Books Week [September 26–October 3, 1998] is a time to celebrate literature and examine the roots of intolerance and ignorance that fuel efforts to censor the arts and free expression. Book censorship is neither infrequent nor an issue of the past. Books with clear artistic and cultural merit are still challenged frequently by those who want to control what others read.

But . . . is book banning really still an issue? Read on . . .

## Examples of Book Banning

In 1998, school officials in Prince William County, Maryland said they would review three books on the school system's summer reading list after a parent complained that the books contain profanity and explicit sex scenes. The books in question were *Nightjohn* by Gary Paulsen, which was on a seventh-grade reading list; *Go Tell It on the Mountain*, by James Baldwin, on a ninth-grade list; and *Slaughterhouse Five* by Kurt Vonnegut Jr., on an 11th grade list.

Two of the three books are no strangers to challenge. During the 1995–96 school year, complaints about *Go Tell It on the Mountain* prompted the removal of the book from a freshman curriculum in Hudson Falls, New York. And *Slaughterhouse Five* has been challenged three times between 1995 and 1998. In two cases, it remained on school reading lists, but in Littlefork, Minnesota in 1997, it was removed from a 12th-grade curriculum.

In other recent cases, Maya Angelou's *I Know Why the Caged Bird Sings* was removed from a ninth-grade English curriculum in Anne Arundel County,

Reprinted, with permission, from the American Civil Liberties Union online publication *Banned Books Week*, September 26–October 3, 1998, at www.aclu.org/issues/freespeech/bbwind.html.

Maryland in 1997, then put back on the condition that teachers warn parents of its content.

## Censorship of Gay and Lesbian Issues

A particular target for censorship are books on gay and lesbian issues. In June 1997, a Republican state legislator introduced a "no promo homo" bill that would make it a felony for any person to provide a minor with material that "condones or advocates . . . alternate lifestyles" without the child's parent first giving consent. The proposed bill would require any group or individual to obtain written parental permission before "disseminating" such information. The bill's sponsor did not explain what he meant by "alternate lifestyles," although a parent testifying in favor of the bill said he was alarmed that books such as Leslea Newman's *Heather Has Two Mommies* are available at local libraries.

In December 1997, answering a show of strong support from students, a Jefferson County, Kentucky school district committee rejected some parents' requests that the district ban three novels by a prominent gay author. "I just don't think we can have a controlled, censored classroom," said Manual High student Stacy Riger, 17, one of about two dozen people who spoke at the meeting. "We definitely can't hide these different lifestyles from our young people by pretending they don't exist."

The books in question are titled *Invisible Life*, *Just As I Am* and *This Too Shall Pass*. The novels by E. Lynn Harris are part of Central High School English teacher Dee Hawkins' classroom collection that her students, in grades 9–12, are allowed to check out to fulfill class reading requirements. Hawkins said she explained to her students that the books have realistic language and mature scenes.

In 1997, the American Civil Liberties Union (ACLU) of Texas sent out an open records request to all Texas school districts to learn which books were challenged or banned between August 1995 and March 1997. From 875 school districts that responded, the ACLU found that more than 220 titles by 142 authors were challenged, including the classic *My Friend Flicka*.

A total of 73 titles were removed from libraries in 30 school districts. One of the books—*We All Fall Down* by Robert Cormier—was removed

> *"A particular target for censorship are books on gay and lesbian issues."*

from two libraries, while some school libraries banned more than one book, according to the ACLU.

In addition to the books removed from library shelves, 11 titles were removed from the curriculum in 10 school districts. Reasons for challenges included "objectionable language" and "descriptions of abuse." The most commonly challenged authors were Judy Blume, Robert Cormier, Christopher Pike and R.L. Stine.

## Censorship in Bookstores

Libraries and schools are not the only places where censorship can be found. In 1998, an Alabama grand jury indicted Barnes & Noble's bookstore for selling *Radiant Identities* by Jock Sturges and *Age of Innocence* by David Hamilton, both targets of a national censorship campaign by conservative groups.

Earlier in 1998, officials in Tennessee indicted a Barnes & Noble bookstore on similar charges over Sturges and Hamilton art books. The store fought the ban but later agreed to display the books wrapped in plastic and available only on bookshelves higher than five feet. The Alabama case is now pending in the courts.

> *"Permitting restraints on literature sets the stage for attacks on all expression that is artistically or politically controversial."*

Attorneys general in Louisiana and Missouri, and a district attorney in Pennsylvania, have all declined to press charges over the sale of Sturges' and Hamilton's books, saying they did not find the photographs obscene.

## Setting the Stage for Further Attacks

The ACLU opposes all forms of censorship. For more than 200 years the right to choose what we see and hear and read has been one of our most cherished freedoms. Permitting restraints on literature sets the stage for attacks on all expression that is artistically or politically controversial or that portrays unpleasant realities of life.

Censorship today comes in many forms, from challenges to school reading lists to emerging issues of library filtering and blocking of the Internet. Whenever a school board or any other government entity limits your right to decide what you want to see, hear or read, that is censorship.

# Speech Codes Threaten Free Speech on College Campuses

by Alan Charles Kors

**About the author:** *Alan Charles Kors is a professor of history at the University of Pennsylvania and coauthor of* The Shadow University: The Betrayal of Liberty on America's Campuses.

Combatants in the culture wars of today's contemporary universities generally focus on issues of curriculum and scholarship, and critics of these prevailing practices have a great deal to target: a so-called multiculturalism that generally is merely a celebration of the cultural Left, wherever it is found; the spread of a pedagogy that seeks disciples rather than critically minded inquirers; the elevation by literary studies of pathology into high theory; the degradation of whole fields of the humanities and social sciences into tendentious "oppression studies"; and scholarship in which one no longer can distinguish between parody and the real thing.

These are not my themes today, however, because of the very phrases that I was forced to use to describe them—combatants, curriculum, scholarship, and critics—all of which denote agents and phenomena that appear in the open, subject to debate. Universities have personnel committees and curricular committees with, almost everywhere, college-wide participation by scholars and teachers who know better and are free to act, but who simply have abandoned their intellectual responsibilities. . . .

Folly without coercive power is not the direct enemy of liberty. Rather, those things that threaten free and open debate and those things that threaten academic freedom are the direct enemy of liberty. Such threats exist most dangerously at universities not in curriculum and scholarship, but in the new university *in loco parentis* (the university standing in the place of parents), where our nation's colleges and universities, across the board, are teaching contempt for

Excerpted from Alan Charles Kors, "The Betrayal of Liberty on America's Campuses," Bradley Lecture delivered at the American Enterprise Institute, Washington, D.C., October 5, 1998. For the full text, see www.aie.org/bradley/bl100598.htm. Reprinted by permission of the author.

liberty and its components: freedom of expression and inquiry; individual rights and responsibilities over group rights and entitlements; equal justice under law; and the rights of private conscience. *That* assault upon liberty is occurring not in the sunlight of open decisions and advertised agendas, but in the shadows of an unaccountable middle-administration that has been given coercive authority over the lives, speech, consciences, and voluntary individuation and association of students.

## Speech Codes

Almost all colleges and universities, for example, have "harassment" policies that prohibit selective "verbal behavior" or "verbal conduct," but almost none has the honesty to call these "speech codes." These policies, adopted from employment law and catastrophic for universities, are applied to faculty and students, the latter not even being employees of a university, but, in fact, its clients. The core of these codes is the prohibition of the creation of "a hostile or offensive environment," with the remarkable variations and embellishments that follow from Thomas Hobbes's observation that to the learned it is given to be learnedly foolish. Within very recent times, Bowdoin College chose to outlaw jokes and ways of telling stories "experienced by others as harassing." Brown University banned verbal behavior that produced "feelings of impotence . . . anger . . . or disenfranchisement . . . [whether] intentional or unintentional." Colby prohibited speech that caused loss of "self-esteem." The University of Connecticut prohibited "inconsiderate jokes," "stereotyping," and even "inappropriately directed laughter." Indeed, a student at Sarah Lawrence College recently was convicted of laughing at something that someone else said, and was ordered as a condition of remaining in the college, for his laughter, to read a book entitled *Homophobia on Campus*, see a movie about "homophobia," and write a paper about "homophobia." Rutgers University included within the forbidden and "heinous act" of harassment, "communication" that is "in any manner likely to cause annoyance or alarm," which causes *me* a great deal of annoyance *and* alarm. The University of Maryland–College Park outlaws not only "idle chatter of a sexual nature" and "comments or questions about the sensuality of a person," but pointedly explains that these verbal behaviors "do not necessarily have to be specifically directed at an individual to constitute sexual harassment." Expression goes well beyond the verbal, however, because the University of Maryland also prohibits "gestures . . . that are expressive of an idea, opinion, or emotion," including "sexual looks such as leering and ogling with suggestive overtones; licking lips or teeth; holding or eating food provocatively."

At Carnegie Mellon University, a student called his female opponent in an

> *"Bowdoin College chose to outlaw jokes and ways of telling stories 'experienced by others as harassing.'"*

election for the Graduate Student Organization a "megalomaniac." He was charged with sexual harassment. The Dean of Students explained the deeper meaning of calling a woman a megalomaniac, citing a vast body of what he termed feminist "victim theory" on the the plaintiff's behalf, and the associate provost submitted a brief that stated, "I have no doubt that this has created a hostile environment which impacts Lara's productivity as a student leader and as a graduate student."

> *"[West Virginia University's speech code] outlawed specific religious inner convictions about sexuality."*

Many universities, such as Berkeley itself, no less, adopted speech codes that outlawed "fighting words." That term is taken from the U.S. Supreme Court decision of the 1940s, *Chaplinsky v. New Hampshire* (a decision surely mooted by later Supreme Court decisions), in which, leftists take note, the unprotected fighting word was, of all things, "fascist." Many universities also leave the determination of whether something was a fighting word or created a hostile environment to the plaintiff. Thus, the University of Puget Sound states that harassment "depends on the point of view of the person to whom the conduct is unwelcome." The City University of New York warns that "sexual harassment is not defined by intentions, but by its impact on the subject." "No one," Bowdoin College warns, "is entitled to engage in behavior that is experienced by others as harassing." At the University of Connecticut, criticising someone's limits of tolerance toward the speech of others is itself harassment: its code bans "attributing objections to any of the above [instances of harassment] to 'hypersensitivity' of the targeted individual or group."

## Codes Applied Unequally

West Virginia University prohibited, among many other things, "insults, humor, jokes, and/or anecdotes that belittle or demean an individual's or a groups' sexuality or sex," and, try this one on for vagueness, "inappropriate displays of sexually suggestive objects or pictures which may include but are not limited to posters, pin-ups, and calendars." If applied equally, of course, such a policy would leave no sex or race safe in its conversations or humor, let alone in its artistic taste, but such policies never are applied equally. Thus, students at West Virginia received the official policies of the "Executive Officer for Social Justice," who stated the institutional orthodoxy about "homophobia" and "sexism." The Officer of Social Justice warned that "feelings" about gays and lesbians could not become "attitudes": "Regardless of how a person feels about others, negative actions or attitudes based on misconceptions and/or ignorance constitute prejudice, which contradicts everything for which an institution of higher leaning stands." Among those prejudices it listed "heterosexism . . . the assumption that everyone is heterosexual, or, if they aren't, they should be." This, of course, outlawed specific religious inner convictions about sexuality. Because everyone had the right to be free from "harassment," the policy specified "behaviors to avoid." These prohibitions affected speech and voluntary associations based upon beliefs. Thus, "DO NOT [in capital letters] tolerate 'jokes' which are potentially injurious to gays, lesbians and bisexuals. . . . DO NOT determine whether you will interact with someone by virtue of his or her sexual orientation." The policy also commanded specific prescriptions: "value alternate lifestyles . . . challenge homophobic remarks . . . [and] use language that is not gender specific. . . . Instead of referring to anyone's romantic partner as 'girlfriend' or 'boyfriend,' use positive generic terms such as a 'friend,' 'lover,' or 'partner.' Speak of your own romantic partner similarly." The "homophobia" policy ended with the warning that "harassment" or "discrimination" based on sexual preference was subject to penalties that ranged "from reprimand . . . to expulsion and termination, and including public service and educational remediation." "Educational remediation," note well, is an academic euphemism for thought reform. Made aware of what their own university was doing, a coalition of faculty members threatened to expose West Virginia University for its obvious violations of the state and federal constitutions, and to sue the administration if need be. The University has removed the offending codes from its freshmen orientation packages and from its website. We shall see if it has removed them from its operational policies. . . .

## A Repressive Atmosphere

Many in the academy insist that the entire phenomenon labeled "political correctness" is the mythical fabrication of opponents of "progressive" change. The authors of an American Association of University Professors' special committee report, the "Statement on the 'Political Correctness' Controversy" (1991), insisted, without irony, that claims of "political correctness" were merely smokescreens to hide the true agenda of such critics—a racist and sexist desire to thwart the aspirations of minorities and women in the academic enterprise.

It is, in fact, almost inconceivable that anyone of good faith could live on a college campus unaware of the repression, legal inequality, intrusions into private conscience, and malignant double standards that hold sway there. In the Left's history of McCarthyism, the firing or dismissal of one professor or student, the inquisition into the private beliefs of one individual, let alone the demands for a demonstration of fealty to community standards, stand out as intolerable oppressions that coerced people into silence, hypocrisy, betrayal, and tyranny.

> *"It is . . . almost inconceivable that anyone of good faith could live on a college campus unaware of the repression [and] legal inequality."*

In fact, in today's assault on liberty on college campuses, there is not a small number of cases, speech codes, nor apparatuses of repression and thought reform. Number aside, however, a climate of repression succeeds not by statistical frequency, but by sapping the courage, autonomy, and conscience of individuals who otherwise might remember or revive what liberty could be.

## The Right of Never Being Offended

Most students respect disagreement and difference, and they do not bring charges of harassment against those whose opinions or expressions "offend" them. The universities themselves, however, encourage such charges to be brought. At almost every college and university, students deemed members of "historically oppressed groups"—above all, women, blacks, gays, and Hispanics—are informed during orientations that their campuses are teeming with illegal or intolerable violations of their "right" not to be offended. To believe many new-student orientations would be to believe that there was a racial or sexual bigot, to borrow the mocking phrase of McCarthy's critics, "under every bed." At almost every college and university, students are presented with lists of a vast array of places to which they should submit charges of such verbal "harassment," and they are promised "victim support," "confidentiality," and sympathetic understanding when they file such complaints.

*"What an extraordinary power to give to administrative tribunals: the prerogative to punish the free speech and expression of people."*

What an astonishing expectation to give to students: the belief that, if they belong to a protected category and have the correct beliefs, they have a right to four years of never being offended. What an extraordinary power to give to administrative tribunals: the prerogative to punish the free speech and expression of people to whom they assign the stains of historical oppression, while being free, themselves, to use whatever rhetoric they wish against the bearers of such stains. While the world looks at issues of curriculum and scholarship, above all, to analyze and evaluate American colleges and universities, it is, in fact, the silencing and punishment of belief, expression, and individuality that ought to concern yet more deeply those who care about what universities are and could be. Most cases never reach the public, because most individuals accused of "verbal" harassment sadly (but understandably) accept plea-bargains that diminish their freedom but spare them Draconian penalties, including expulsion. Those settlements almost invariably involve "sensitivity training," an appalling term, "training," to hear in matters of the human mind and spirit. Even so, the files on prosecutions under speech codes are, alas, overflowing.

## Thought Reform

"Settlements," by the way, are one of the best-kept and most frightening secrets of American academic life, almost always assigned with an insistence upon confidentiality. They are nothing less than an American version of thought reform from benighted offender into a politically correct bearer, in fact or in appearance, of an ideology that is the regnant orthodoxy of our universities *in loco parentis*.

From this perspective, American history is a tale of the oppression of all "others" by white, heterosexual, Eurocentric males, punctuated by the struggles of the oppressed. "Beneficiaries" see their lives as good and as natural, and falsely view America as a boon to humankind. Worse, most "victims" of "oppression" accept the values of their oppressors. A central task of education, then, is to "demystify" such arbitrary power. Whites, males, and heterosexuals must recognize and renounce the injustice of their "privilege." Nonwhites, women, gays, and lesbians must recognize and struggle against their victimization, both in their beliefs and in their behaviors.

> *"History has taught us the nightmare of violating the ultimate refuges of self-consciousness, conscience, and private beliefs."*

Such "demystification" has found a welcome home in a large number of courses in the humanities and social sciences, but for the true believers, this is insufficient, because most courses remain optional, many professors resist the temptation to proselytize, and students, for the most part, choose majors that take them far from oppression studies.

Indeed, students forever disappoint the ideologues. Men and women generally see themselves neither as oppressor nor oppressed, and, far from engaging in class warfare, often quite love each other. Most women refuse to identify themselves as "feminists." Group-identity centers—although they can rally support at moments of crisis—attract few students overall, because invitees busily go about the business of learning, making friends, pursuing interests, and seeking love—all the things that 18-to-22-year-olds have done from time immemorial. Attendance at group-identity organizations is often minuscule as a percentage of the intended population, and militant leaders complain endlessly about "apathy." Whites don't feel particularly guilty about being white, and almost no designated "victims" adopt truly radical politics. Most undergraduates unabashedly seek their portion of American freedom, legal equality, and bounty. What to do with such benighted students? Increasingly, the answer to that question is to use the *in loco parentis* apparatus of the university to reform their private consciences and minds. For the generation that once said, "Don't trust anyone *over* 30," the motto now is "Don't trust anyone *under* 30." Increasingly, Offices of Student Life, Residence Offices, and residence advisors have become agencies of progressive social engineering whose mission is to bring students to mandatory political enlightenment.

## Violating Private Conscience and Belief

Such practices violate far more than honest education. Recognition of the sanctity of conscience is the single most essential respect given to individual autonomy. There are purely practical arguments for the right to avoid self-incrimination or to choose religious (or other) creeds, but there is none deeper than restraining power from intruding upon the privacy of the self. Universities and colleges that commit the scandal of sentencing students (and faculty) to "sensitivity therapy" do not even permit individuals to choose their therapists. The Christian may not consult his or her chosen counselor, but must follow the regime of the social worker selected by the Women's Center or by the Office of Student Life.

Examine, for example, a plea bargain rejected by a student at the University of Pennsylvania in April of 1992. The student took his chances with the ordeal of a hearing, where he was acquitted of sexual harassment. It took courage to take that chance when accepting a plea bargain would have ended the matter. The proposed settlement, typical of what occurs at so many universities (now you will know what is meant by "educational not punitive settlements") was equally chilling in its command over time and private conscience, and in its authoritarian and

> *"Speech codes merely formalize the will to censor and to devalue liberty of thought and speech."*

partisan supervision. An attorney in the Office of General Counsel confirmed that he had "signed off on scores" of identical settlements:

> You are to participate in a comprehensive program on sexual harassment, except for the time you are attending classes . . . or [at] employment. Said programming shall include . . . assignments . . . each week in which classes are in session through the Spring 1992 term. You [must] present written evidence of completion of assignments, and a satisfactory performance must be documented by Elena DiLapi, Director of the Women's Center, or her representative, before your transcript can be released.

From the Inquisition to Soviet psychiatry, history has taught us the nightmare of violating the ultimate refuges of self-consciousness, conscience, and private beliefs. In Friedrich von Schiller's *Don Carlos*, Alba observes that even "A slave can keep his feelings from a king. It is his only right." The final horror of *1984* was the Party's goal of changing Winston's consciousness against his will. The song of the "peat bog soldiers" sent by the Nazis to work until they died was, appropriately, "Die Gedanken sind frei"—"Thoughts are free"—for that truly is the final atom of liberty. No moral person would pursue another human being there. Colleges and universities do. . . .

## Repressing Unpopular Speech

Speech codes, with all of their formal clauses, are in fact a parody of the rule of law, but we should not obsess on them. Freedom dies in the heart and will before it dies in the law. Speech codes merely formalize the will to censor and to devalue liberty of thought and speech. Even without invoking codes, universities have found ways to silence or to chill freedom of opinion and expression. Indeed, defenders of free speech at our colleges and universities become tarred by the sorts of speech they must defend if they wish to defend freedom in general. No one who defends trial by jury over popular justice in a murder trial is called a defender of murder; such a person is seen, by all, as a defender of trial by jury. The defender of free speech, however, is forever being told, on American campuses, that he or she is seeking, specifically, to make the campus safe for "racism," "sexism," or "homophobia." That is true if what one means is that the defender of free speech seeks to make the campus safe for the expression of all views, and for the clash of visions, ideas, and passions. The issue is not the protection of this or that person's rights by our subjective criteria of who deserves freedom, but the protection of freedom itself.

The speech-code provisions of harassment policies are merely symptoms of the willful assault on liberty on our campuses: the suppression and punishment of controversial and unpopular ideas; the banning of terms that offend listeners invested with special rights; and the outlawing of discourse that, in the eyes of the defenders of the new orthodoxies, "creates a hostile environment." The essential purpose of a speech code is to repress speech. It may serve other ends, such as making its framers feel moral, powerful, or simply safe from the attacks of those who would criticize them. It also demonstrates, for all to observe, who controls the symbolic environment of a place—a heady feeling for the wielders of power, and a demonstration, of course, that also succeeds in silencing others.

If colleges and universities were beset not by the current "political orthodoxy," but by some other claim for the unequal assignment of protections and rights—"religious orthodoxy," or "patriotic orthodoxy," for example—victims of those calls for repression and double standards would find the evil obvious. Imagine secular, skeptical, or Left-wing faculty and students confronted by a religious harassment code that prohibited "denigration" of evangelical or Catholic beliefs, or that made the classroom or campus a space where evangelical or Catholic students must be protected against feeling "intimidated," "offended," or, by their own subjective experience, victims of "a hostile environment." Imagine a university of patriotic "loyalty oaths" where Leftists were deemed responsible for the tens of millions of victims of Communism, and where postmodernists were prohibited from creating a hostile environment for patriots, or from offending that "minority" of individuals who are descended from Korean War or Vietnam War veterans. Imagine, as

> *"The essential purpose of a speech code is to repress speech."*

well, that for every "case" that became public, there were scores or hundreds of cases in which the "offender" or "victimizer," desperate to preserve a job or gain a degree, accepted a confidential plea-bargain that included a semester's or a year's reeducation in "religious sensitivity" or "patriotic sensitivity" seminars run by the university's "Evangelical Center," "Patriotic Center," or "Office of Religious and Patriotic Compliance." What praise of liberty we would see then.

Imagine a campus on which being denounced for "irreligious bigotry" or "un-Americanism" carried the same stigma that being denounced for "racism," "sexism," and "homophobia" now carries in the academic world, so that in such hearings or trials, the burden of proof invariably fell upon the "offender." The common sign at pro-choice rallies, "Keep your rosaries off our ovaries," would be prima facie evidence of language used as a weapon to degrade and marginalize, and the common term of abuse, "born-again bigot," would be compelling evidence of the choice to create a hostile environment for evangelicals. What panegyrics to liberty and free expression we would hear in opposition to any proposed code to protect the "religious" or the "patriotic" from "offense" and "incivility." Yet what deafening silence we have heard, in these times, in the campus acceptance of the speech provisions of so-called harassment codes.

> *"Universities, for their own partisan reasons, have chosen to betray the human vision of freedom and legal equality."*

## The Struggle for Liberty and Equality

The goal of a speech code, then, is to suppress speech one doesn't like. The goal of liberty and equal justice is to permit us to live in a complex but peaceful world of difference, disagreement, debate, moral witness, and efforts of persuasion—without coercion and violence. Liberty and legal equality are hard-won, precious, and, indeed—because the social world is often discomforting—profoundly complex and troublesome ways of being human. They require, for their sustenance, men and women who would abhor their own power of censorship and their own special legal privileges as much as they abhor those of others. In enacting and enforcing speech codes, universities, for their own partisan reasons, have chosen to betray the human vision of freedom and legal equality. It was malignant to impose or permit such speech codes; to deny their oppressive effects while living in the midst of those effects is beyond the moral pale.

On virtually any college campus, for all of its rules of "civility" and all of its prohibitions of "hostile environment," assimilationist black men and women live daily with the terms "Uncle Tom" and "Oreo" said with impunity, while their tormenters live with special protections from offense. White students daily hear themselves, their friends, and their parents denounced as "racists" and "oppressors," while their tormenters live with special protections from offense. Believing Christians hear their beliefs ridiculed and see their sacred symbols traduced—virtually nothing, in the name of freedom, may not be said against them in the classroom, at rallies, and in personal encounters—while their tormenters live with special protection from offense. Men hear their sex abused, find themselves blamed for all the evils of the world, and enter classrooms whose very goal is to make them feel discomfort, while their tormenters live with special protections from "a hostile environment."

It is our liberty, above all else, that defines us as human beings, capable of ethics and responsibility. The struggle for liberty on American campuses is one of the defining struggles of the age in which we find ourselves. A nation that does not educate in freedom will not survive in freedom, and will not even know when it has lost it. Individuals too often convince themselves that they are caught up in moments of history that they cannot affect. That history, however, is made by their will and moral choices. There is a moral crisis in higher education. It will not be resolved unless we choose and act to resolve it.

# A Flag-Burning Amendment Would Threaten Free Speech

by Jamin B. Raskin

**About the author:** *Jamin B. Raskin is a professor of constitutional law at American University's Washington College of Law.*

On February 13, 1997, House Rules Chairman Gerald Solomon (R-NY) and Rep. William Lipinski (D-IL) introduced H.J. Res. 54, a proposed constitutional Amendment that reads as follows:

> Congress shall have power to prohibit the physical desecration of the flag of the United States.

Congressmen Solomon and Lipinski thus seek to become authors of the first constitutional amendment since Prohibition designed to put people in jail and the first in our history to strip First Amendment freedoms from the Bill of Rights. Congress should act with common sense and reject the first amendment to the First Amendment.

The Amendment is explicitly aimed at eviscerating the Supreme Court's 1989 decision in *Texas v. Johnson*, which struck down a one-year criminal sentence and $2,000 fine imposed by Texas on Revolutionary Communist Party member Gregory Johnson, who burned an American flag outside the Republican National Convention in 1984.

## The Bedrock Principle

Justice Brennan's opinion for the Court in *Texas v. Johnson* stated the idea that lies at the heart of the First Amendment: "If there is a bedrock principle underlying the First Amendment, it is that Government may not prohibit the expression of an idea simply because society finds the idea itself offensive or disagreeable." This principle "is not dependent on the particular mode in which one chooses to express an idea," Justice Brennan wrote, and "We have not rec-

Excerpted from Jamin B. Raskin, memo on the proposed flag amendment to the U.S. Constitution, March 30, 1997, published on the ACLU Freedom Network's online publication "In Congress," at www.aclu.org/congress/103309/a.html. Reprinted by permission of the author.

ognized an exception to this principle even where our flag has been involved."

Significantly, Justice Brennan refused to cede the ground of patriotism to those who wanted to lock up Gregory Johnson. "Our toleration of criticism such as Johnson's is a sign and source of our strength. Indeed, one of the proudest images of our flag, the one immortalized in our own national anthem, is of the bombardment it survived at Fort McHenry. It is the nation's resilience, not its rigidity, that Texas sees reflected in the flag—and it is that resilience that we reassert today."

In words that today's flag-enshriners should take to heart, Justice Brennan concluded: "We do not consecrate the flag by punishing its desecration, for in doing so we dilute the freedom that this cherished emblem represents."

> *"Government may not prohibit the expression of an idea simply because society finds the idea itself offensive or disagreeable."*

The Supreme Court's ruling should have put an end to the matter, but instead we have been embroiled in flag wars ever since. Congress debated and rejected the Flag Amendment twice, once in 1990 and then again in 1995. The Republic has survived in the meantime.

Now the Constitutional amendment is back again, its advocates brandishing public opinion polls as their one and only argument. But a 1995 Peter Hart poll found that a majority of Americans *opposed* the Flag Amendment by a margin of 52% to 38% when they learned that it would be the first in history to cut back on the First Amendment freedom of expression.

## Why a Flag Amendment?

Flag Amendment backers want to carve out an exception to the First Amendment, but no one can say why this constitutional change is necessary. There is no epidemic of flag-burning in the country, nor has the country experienced any loss of patriotism or respect for Old Glory since *Texas v. Johnson* was decided. Published reports suggest that, in a nation of a quarter of a billion people, there have been fewer than five flag-burnings a year since the Court's decision. One is more likely to be in an earthquake or to win the lottery than to be subjected to a political flag-burning.

Moreover, Congress doesn't need the Amendment to "protect" the flag that flies above the Capitol building or on other public property. Congress *owns* those flags, and any attempt to burn them would constitute criminal trespass, destruction of public property, arson, reckless endangerment and potentially numerous other offenses. What the Amendment would do is "protect" flags from their own rightful owners, in essence nationalizing control over tens of millions of pieces of private property.

Ironically, with the number of flag-hostile groups dwindling to near zero, nothing presents a greater threat to the physical safety of our flag population today than passage of the Flag Amendment itself, which would undoubtedly trigger a rash of flag-burnings by political protestors of one stripe or another. Many Americans would dust off the slogan of another time-honored American flag and say: "Don't tread on me." If the object of the Amendment is to reduce further the tiny number of flags put to flame, then this is a counterproductive strategy. Indeed, the Amendment would be a much greater threat to the physical safety of flags than Gregory Johnson ever was.

The Amendment represents a fashion in empty symbolic politics, the kind on display when the House of Representatives voted to endorse the Ten Commandments on March 5, 1996. The Flag Amendment's proponents have appealed principally to veterans, who have served our country and shown it great love. But Congress would be returning the favor a lot more honorably by addressing the urgent needs that veterans have rather than practicing constitutional thought control.

If passed, the Amendment will be followed by enactment of a new federal statute criminalizing *flag desecration*, but there is dangerous ambiguity about the meaning of its two key terms: "desecration" and "flag."

## What Does "Desecration" Mean?

"Desecration" is a religious concept. According to Webster's, its primary meaning is "to violate the sanctity of," to "profane." The Flag Amendment implicitly constitutionalizes "the flag" as America's sacred or divine object.

Religious and secular Americans alike may think twice about consecrating the flag as our national civic religion. For Christians, Jews and others who follow the Old Testament, establishing the flag as an untouchable and sacred symbol surely offends the First and Second *Commandments*, which forbid idol worship and graven images, divine directives that cannot be reconciled with the pious and idolatrous concept of "flag desecration.". . .

Some people may think that flag-desecration simply means flag-burning, but that equation doesn't work. As the Court pointed out in *Texas v. Johnson*, flag-burning is actually *recommended* by Congress when a flag gets old. The apparent intention of the Flag Amendment's proposers is not to keep flags from being burned but to keep them from being burned prematurely.

Furthermore, the flag protection movements that have sprung up over the last century have been careful to define desecration far more broadly

> *"There have been fewer than five flag-burnings a year since [1989]."*

than the mere act of burning. The principal target of early-twentieth century flag desecration statutes was the use of the flag in commercial advertising. Given the rarity of political flag-burnings, commercial advertising today clearly will be the most pervasive offender of the new legal regime. Two dormant federal flag-respect statutes already ban any use of the flag in commercial advertising. These laws have gone unenforced only because of First Amendment case law that will be rendered obsolete by the Flag Amendment, and these statutes will immediately spring back to life. Thus, if the Amendment passes, presumably Chevrolet, Ralph Lauren, Speedo, and Tommy Hilfiger would all have to change their flag-based trade dress and turn their existing inventories over as criminal contraband. No longer could the flag appear in a used car salesman's billboard, on a pair of boxers, on Tommy aftershave lotion, or any other piece of merchandise. . . .

> *"Religious and secular Americans alike may think twice about consecrating the flag as our national civic religion."*

The Flag Amendment will also end up criminalizing a lot of artistic expression, as many members of Congress have made clear in their denuciations of particular artistic works. Flag desecration is flag desecration, whether committed on the street or in a museum or in a book of photographs or drawings. Think of the great artists who have incorporated the flag or parts of it in their work: Jasper Johns in his series of famous and beautiful flag paintings, Bruce Springsteen's great album "Born in the USA," Kate Millett's mixed media treatment of the flag in "The American Dream Goes to Pot," Faith Ringgold's "The Flag Is Bleeding," and Erika Rothenburg's "Flag Trophy." Countless movies and documentaries have included real or fictionalized footage of flag-burnings and other forms of flag "desecration." The most recent, of course, is *The People v. Larry Flynt,* in which actor Woody Harrelson, playing Flynt, appears in court wearing an American flag-diaper. Would Harrelson and the movie's producer and director be subject to arrest and imprisonment for conspiracy to commit flag desecration? The Flag Amendment will thrust government into direct policing and censorship of art and film, a result completely offensive in a free democratic society.

## What Does "Flag" Mean?

Proponents of the Amendment act as if it is self-evident what a "flag" is. But recall that "the flag," unlike the Lincoln Memorial or the White House, is not a single physical object existing at one place. In cultural and political terms, "the flag" is simply a schematic color pattern and design, universally reproducible in cotton, paper, birthday cake icing, magic marker, condoms, and any other medium. But the Flag Amendment converts this democratic public-domain design into the exclusive trademark of the State, making it available for use only under a government license.

The problems of policing the government's new trademark are mind-boggling and ultimately silly. In a freedom-loving country like America, citizens will find ingenious ways to test the boundaries of official thought control. Imagine prosecutors and judges trying to sort out whether the following are acts of criminal flag desecration or free speech:

• Critics of the U.S. Postal Service burn flag stamps to protest inefficiency at the post office.

• Dissenters on-line project the exact image of the flag on millions of computer screens through the Internet and stage a virtual "burning" of the "flag" image. (A flag-burning Web-Site on-line already exists!)

• Knowing that federal law requires old flags to be burned, Gregory Johnson and friends urge people to throw their worn-out flags into a huge bonfire and then light it—in front of the Republican National Convention in the year 2000. Others afraid of being arrested burn homemade American flags missing one star.

These slippery-slope antics will force courts to invent ever-more-delicate distinctions between flag desecration and free speech. A tremendous amount of time and judicial resources will be wasted on defining the exact dimensions of the government's trademark rights in the flag.

## The Dangerous Arbitrariness of the Flag Amendment

It is not at all clear why we should choose to criminalize this kind of symbolic offense over others. Enactment of this amendment will quickly invite similar types of proposals:

• With equal force, people could demand that we amend the Constitution to allow Congress to ban display of the Confederate flag, which is to many people the more obvious and threatening symbol of violent destruction of the Union. No one died when Greg Johnson burned a flag in 1984, but hundreds of thousands died because the Confederate flag flew on our land. Indeed, there is a clear connection between American flag-burning and Confederate flag display: the very first recorded flag-burners were Confederate sympathizers who in 1861 ignited Old Glory in traitorous protest rallies in Richmond, Memphis and Liberty, Mississippi.

• With equal force, people could demand an amendment to allow Congress to ban the swastika, a symbol which tens of thousands of Americans died to save us from and which cost the lives of millions.

• With equal force, people could demand an amendment to allow Congress to criminalize cross-burning. The KKK has burned a lot more crosses than the RCP has burned flags, and cross-burning sends a message of terror to racial minorities.

*"The Flag Amendment will also end up criminalizing a lot of artistic expression."*

• With equal force, people could demand an amendment to allow the criminalization of hate speech, pornography, blasphemous speech, idolatry, or any other kind of offensive speech.

The ACLU opposes all forms of censorship and thought control, and wants to stop America from heading down that road before we all lose our most precious freedoms of thought, conscience and expression.

Thought control is a dangerous business that runs counter to the whole trajectory of our constitutional development, which has continually given us more liberty rather than less. The flag has thus come to represent freedom, not only to Americans but to people all over the world. The Flag Amendment represents the urge to impose thought control on the American people, and thus threatens to turn our beloved flag into a symbol of repression. We can—and we must—save the integrity of both the Constitution and the flag by stopping the Flag Amendment once and for all.

# Limits on Campaign Spending Threaten Political Speech

by Lamar Alexander

**About the author:** *Lamar Alexander, former governor of Tennessee, was a candidate for the Republican presidential nomination in 1996.*

One wintry day in January, 1776, an unsigned pamphlet appeared on the streets of Philadelphia. Its title was *Common Sense*. In the most inflammatory terms, it urged the American colonists to declare their independence from Britain.

This is what *Common Sense* had to say about the King of England's ancestry: "A French bastard landing with armed bandits, and establishing himself King of England against the consent of the natives. . . ."

This is what *Common Sense* had to say about King George himself. "He hath wickedly broken through every moral and human obligation, trampled nature and conscience beneath his feet; and by a steady and constitutional spirit of insolence and cruelty, procured for himself universal hatred."

Thomas Paine wrote *Common Sense*. Paine's revolutionary rhetoric confounded the political class, but it struck a chord among the colonists. *Common Sense* sold more than 100,000 copies and provided the spark that lead to the American declaration of independence from Britain.

## The Urge to Regulate Political Speech

Tom Paine was lucky that King George wasn't running for reelection in 1776. Because if he had been, and today's so-called campaign finance reformers had been around, the Federal Election Commission would have regulated the pamphlets Tom Paine printed.

If there had been elections in 1776, the campaign finance regulations being proposed today would have declared *Common Sense* "express advocacy" that

Reprinted, by permission, from Lamar Alexander, "Should Tom Paine Have Filed with the FEC? The Loss of Common Sense in Campaign Finance Reform," speech delivered at the Cato Institute, Washington, D.C., January 21, 1998.

is, political speech that can be controlled by the government. Indeed, to print his pamphlet Paine and his fellow supporters of independence would have to form a political action committee—called, say, "People for the Overthrow of the Mad King"—file the requisite forms, restrict their contributions, even add a disclaimer. Under some versions of reforms being proposed, they would have to give the King equal time.

In the same way, Harriet Beecher Stowe would certainly have been in trouble if these reformers had been around in 1862 when Abraham Lincoln was elected president. It was Mrs. Stowe who wrote *Uncle Tom's Cabin*, a book that was so influential that when Lincoln met her in 1863 he called her, "The little lady who made this big war." Had Mrs. Stowe put out a new edition of *Uncle Tom's Cabin* in 1860 that said on its cover "Mr. Lincoln is a fine man," today's reformers would have swept her advocacy of the abolition of slavery under the scope of federal regulation.

Tom Paine, Harriet Beecher Stowe and countless others have rallied like-minded Americans to their causes and, by doing so, changed the course of our history. But they were what today's reformers would regard as problems in need of correction. That is, "special interests" in need of regulation.

> *"Most Americans have missed the significance of the campaign finance debate because it seems so far-removed from them."*

The rage to reform political campaigns comes and goes with the frequency and ferocity of El Niño. Every couple of decades or so, it seems, a hot-air front of self-designated "reformers," editorial page editors and Sunday morning talk show pundits gathers force to complain about the corrupting influence of money in campaigns and the nefarious effects of so-called "special interests."

Such a front is storming through our public debate today. But this one has the potential to leave more destruction in its wake than in years past. Most Americans have missed the significance of the campaign finance debate because it seems so far-removed from them. It is conducted in Washingtonese, all that talk about "hard" and "soft" money, about rule this or section that, about which credit card Al Gore used when he made phone calls from which room of the White House.

## Common Sense and Free Speech

What I want to talk about is much bigger than campaign finance reform. I want to talk about common sense and free speech; about preserving the right of Americans like Tom Paine and Harriet Beecher Stowe to petition their government and rally their fellow citizens for political change. Today that right is being threatened by politicians who call themselves reformers; by big guys who find themselves threatened by the speech of little guys.

43

For 24 years, challengers to the Washington establishment have had their political speech hamstrung by contribution and spending limits imposed by an earlier generation of self-styled "reformers." Yesterday's challengers are today's establishment, so many of them are now crafting their own so-called "re-forms"—in other words, rules that will have the effect of protecting the power of the reformers. The arrogant Washington empire is striking back.

> *"The Watergate reforms have proven to be a perfect disaster."*

How did we come to this point? Those who want to make our politics and politicians better through government regulation always trace the source of our problems to money—money in politics. Obviously, if you identify money as the problem, then the solution is to reduce the role of money in campaigns. But that, it turns out, is a little like trying to make your house dust-free. You'll never succeed unless you can make the place airtight—a feat we have conclusively proved is impossible when it comes to eliminating from campaigns the money that makes advocacy possible.

## Disastrous Reforms

In 1974, in an understandable burst of indignation following Watergate, reformers limited the amount of money that could be contributed to federal candidates, and, in the case of presidential candidates, they limited the amount those candidates could spend. If the goal of these new regulations was to attract the largest number of good candidates, give them an opportunity to project their message and give us an opportunity to hear it, the Watergate reforms have proven to be a perfect disaster.

The limits have made fund raising so difficult that many good candidates opt out. The limits have caused campaigns to start ridiculously early so candidates have time to meet enough $1,000 contributors. They have made it less likely that voters will hear the candidates' message. They have given Washington insiders and the national media more say and outsiders less say. The limits protect incumbents and discourage insurgents, and are gradually filling up Congress with the super rich who can afford to spend their own funds. In addition, they have squeezed the life out of campaigns as volunteers discover they have to check with a Washington agency before they can print a campaign slogan on a T-shirt.

Oblivious to this, the reformers are still looking around—and guess what they are seeing? There is still money out there. This time, though, instead of going after candidates directly, they are going after political parties and independent groups.

So, the latest efforts to make the house of politics airtight are aimed at the non-politicians—the modern-day Tom Paines and Harriet Beecher Stowes—whose spending—until now—has been relatively unfettered by government regulation. In fact, if there is one common element to the current so-called "campaign finance reform" proposals it is that they consist of efforts by the regulated—that is, federal politicians—to regulate the unregulated. That is, you and you and you.

The most prominent proposal out there—one endorsed by President Clinton and 48 United States Senators—has even flirted with the idea of banning political action committee contributions to candidates under the guise of eliminating the influence of "special interests." By "special interests," the self-styled reformers mean groups such as the National Association of Realtors, with its 118,000 members, each of whom paid $11.78 to "influence" the elections of 1996—about the cost of one copy of *Uncle Tom's Cabin* at today's prices.

## Trampling on the Freedom of Political Speech

But the most troubling aspect of the so-called reform bills now being considered on Capitol Hill is that they weaken the First Amendment in the very area in which the Founders believed it was most needed. That is, protection of the right to freedom of political speech. The authors of the Constitution did not have in mind the speech rights of pornographers or "performance artists" when they instructed that "Congress shall make no law . . . abridging the freedom of speech." They had in mind citizens with ideas—even unpopular ideas—about how they would govern themselves.

Current campaign finance "reform" proposals trample on this notion by expanding the definition of political speech that can be regulated by the federal government. A long line of Supreme Court cases has established a clear division between political speech that is subject to regulation by government and speech that is not.

As the rules stand today, ads that use express terms—phrases such as "vote for" or "vote against" are known as "express advocacy" and are subject to FEC regulation. Ads that don't use express terms, even if they run during a campaign and refer to one of the candidates—are called "issue advocacy." "Issue advocacy" is outside the realm of government regulation. Examples of this would be the National Rifle Association running ads about preserving the right to bear arms, or the National Association of Realtors with ads about protecting the home mortgage-interest deduction, or the AFL-CIO [American Federation of Labor and Congress of Industrial Organizations] with ads about defeating fast-track trade legislation.

> *"The most troubling aspect of the so-called reform bills . . . is that they weaken the First Amendment."*

Now, here is what the proposed rules would do—they would make the bright line between "express advocacy" and "issue advocacy" not so bright. Groups could cross it and find themselves in trouble by including in an ad or publication a campaign slogan or words that "in context can have no reasonable meaning other" than to advocate the election or defeat of a candidate. It would be left to the FEC to determine what is a "reasonable meaning" and what is not. For example, the words "As read by Abraham Lincoln" on the cover of *Uncle Tom's Cabin*. It would be left to the FEC to determine whether that meant Mrs. Stowe advocated Lincoln's election or not.

This legislation would also prohibit for 60 days prior to an election paid advertising that referred "to one or more clearly identified candidates." This would have made criminals of the two ladies who took out an ad in the newspaper on the eve of the 1972 election to protest President Nixon's bombing of Cambodia.

## Trying to Get Even

There are more than 100 bills, sponsored by over 100 elected officials, being considered in Congress under the pretense of making our democracy better. But ask yourself—If the goal of campaign finance reform is to prevent the corruption of politicians, why would these politicians try so hard to limit the speech of independent interest groups?

I'll tell you why. Purely and simply, it's a case of self protection. After years of being muzzled by spending and contribution limits, many candidates—especially incumbents—are beginning to feel outgunned by independent groups that are not similarly shackled by federal regulations.

I have a little experience on this score myself, so let me see if I can give you an example of how this might work. Let's say, purely hypo-

> *"The U.S. Supreme court ruled that it is impossible to untangle the right to spend freely . . . from the right to speak freely."*

thetically, that I am running for federal office. Say, for instance, I'm in New Hampshire. I'm walking. I'm wearing a plaid shirt. The National Education Association, the teacher's union, sees an opportunity. It doesn't like my support for merit pay for teachers so it decides to spend $100,000 proclaiming that, "Lamar Alexander is one of the 32 national leaders of the radical right leading a crusade against public schools." (This isn't entirely hypothetical. An NEA workshop brochure actually said this.)

You can quickly see why candidates like me would rather the NEA not be able to spend money to say such things. Because I must raise money in $1,000 increments and spend within certain limits, and the NEA is not today subject to such fund raising restrictions, I'm at a real disadvantage in rebutting their "enemies list" charge. That is, I would be if I were interested in rebutting that charge.

This is the dirty little secret behind so-called "campaign finance reform": earlier reforms have put candidates at a big disadvantage in relation to groups like the NEA and the NRA. This is the candidates' chance to get even.

But there is a good reason why previous reformers stopped short of cutting off the speech of independent groups. In the *Buckley vs. Valeo* decision in 1976, the U.S. Supreme Court ruled that it is impossible to untangle the right to spend freely on political campaigns from the right to speak freely. It said that "the concept that government may restrict the speech of some elements of our society in order to enhance the relative voice of others is wholly foreign to the First Amendment."

Yet, restricting the free speech rights of some to enhance the rights of others is exactly what is being attempted today. The reasoning goes like this: candidates and interest groups don't enjoy equal speech rights. The interest groups are outspending us, they're outmaneuvering us and they're outspeaking us. And we're mad as hell and we're not going to take it anymore.

For example, in the first race of 1998, the special election to fill the California congressional seat of the late Representative Walter Capps, the spending of the independent groups, not the candidates, was decisive. In one weekend alone, the Campaign for Working Families, a pro-family, anti-abortion group, spent $100,000 on TV ads—to help a candidate who had raised only $130,000. Another candidate felt compelled to air an ad in response, not to charges raised by his opponent, but to those raised by an independent group. But did all that spending hurt the election? Turnout was 46%—extremely high for a California special election.

A congressman who had been targeted by literature distributed by the National Right-to-Life Committee and the Christian Coalition in 1996 summed up the current frustration among Washington politicians when he said, "It's unfair to voters and candidates to allow third parties to liberally participate in the political process then claim immunities from the rules of engagement."

His solution? To change the so-called "rules of engagement" in order to end the "liberal participation" of independent groups in elections. This is an understandable, though misguided, impulse. Candidates for federal office do face great obstacles in raising the money to make their voices heard and to respond to the charges of their opponents.

I have felt their pain. When I ran for president in 1996, contribution and spending limits forced me to spend 70 percent of my time raising money in amounts no greater than $1000. To raise $10 million during 1995 I had to travel to 250 fundraising events—about one for every campaign day. One million of that $10 million was spent on the costs of complying with the federal rules; another $2.5 million went to pay for the cost of raising the money; much of the rest was eaten up by the long campaign necessary to raise so much money! So, I understand what

> *"Campaigns don't exist for members of Congress . . . or for any other candidate. They exist for voters."*

these office-holders are complaining about. It's as if they are engaged in a spirited game of paint ball, only instead of paint balls the independent groups have real bullets.

There's just one problem: campaigns don't exist for members of Congress, or for me, or for any other candidate. They exist for voters. And the greater the ability of all the contestants to speak freely—whether we like what they have to say or not—the better the quality and the quantity of the choices that the voters will have.

I have a better solution.

## Free Speech and Full Disclosure

1. *More speech, not less.* First, we should banish the phrase "campaign finance reform" from our vocabulary. Its supporters won't acknowledge it, but "campaign finance reform" is a euphemism for government regulation of political speech. And what our campaigns need is more freedom of speech, not less.

2. *The First Amendment Protection Act.* Next, we should do away with the so-called "rules of engagement" and start over. Today I issue a call to each of the 102 frustrated politicians who have sponsored legislation that would enhance their freedom of speech by limiting that of others: Choose free speech instead. The 105th Congress should immediately table all of its so-called "campaign finance reform" bills and introduce in their place the "First Amendment Protection Act."

Unlike the current approach—which [journalist and author] Jonathan Rauch has called "the gobbledygook that interposes gibbering hordes of lawyers and bureaucrats between politicians and voters"—the "First Amendment Protection Act" I propose is based on two simple but powerful concepts: free speech and full disclosure.

> *"Wouldn't it make more common sense if the FEC . . . directed [its energy] toward making sure that voters were kept fully informed?"*

Self-appointed reformers would never suggest that there is too much speech in our politics, yet that is what they are saying when they insist on limiting the money that is spent. The "First Amendment Protection Act" would restore free speech by removing all limits on contributions made by individuals, PACs or political parties to campaigns and PACs. And, it would remove campaign spending limits. Instead, it would require full and prompt disclosure of all contributions.

3. *Electronic full disclosure.* Third, in place of limits, the First Amendment Protection Act would require full and prompt electronic disclosure of all contributions.

Wouldn't it make more common sense if the FEC took all the energy it now spends enforcing contribution and spending limits and directed it toward making sure that voters were kept fully informed about the candidates and their financial backers? California Congressman John Doolittle has sponsored a bill that would require electronic filing of campaign reports with the FEC. It would require reports to be filed every 24 hours during the three months preceding an election. What's more, the Doolittle bill would require the FEC to post all campaign reports on the Internet, where in just a half-hour spent online a voter could learn more about a campaign than by spending a week at the FEC, shuffling through paper.

## No Public Financing or Coerced Contributions

4. *End public financing of presidential campaigns.* By removing campaign contribution limits we will have an added benefit. That is, we will eliminate the rationale for the incestuous system of publicly financing presidential campaigns. The Supreme Court has ruled that the only spending limits that may be placed on presidential campaigns are voluntary ones. Public financing—which the taxpayers have subsidized to the tune of about $900 million over the last two decades—is the "carrot" offered by the federal government to persuade candidates to accept spending limits. Of course, contribution limits make this carrot more like a stick for any candidate in a tax bracket lower than Steve Forbes. Eliminate contribution limits and you eliminate the need for public financing by making it easier for candidates to raise money.

> *"Freedom of speech is one of the handful of ideas that unites us as Americans."*

5. *Stop coerced contributions.* The final real reform in the "First Amendment Protection Act" will be to extend paycheck protection to everybody who earns a wage. There may not be too much money in politics, but there is too much coerced money in politics. The forcible collection of union dues for political advocacy is not free speech. What it is is free money for union bosses. California—and at least three other states—[voted in 1998] on initiatives that would bar corporations and unions from collecting or using money from employees for political purposes without the employee's written consent. This is a rare kind of campaign finance reform—one that people actually care about and that actually works. Congress should make it the law of the land.

## Protecting Freedom of Speech

But let's be realistic. Replacing bogus "campaign finance reform" with these two simple principles—free speech and full disclosure—will require an act of real courage on the part of the Congress. It will require that they ignore the Washington echo chamber of so-called "good government" reformers and editorial page preachers and put their trust in the people to make informed political choices, even if the choices are disagreeable ones.

It is in the marketplace of competing political viewpoints that we will find the leaders and the ideas that will take America well into the 21st century. And if we want the new American century to reflect proudly on that original American century, then we must heed a lesson from our past.

Tom Paine and Harriet Beecher Stowe were successful in changing the course of history because they were free to speak—and their speech rallied people to their causes.

## Free Speech

Freedom of speech is one of the handful of ideas that unites us as Americans; that brings new people to our shores and insures the constant renewal of our republic. A real danger that faces America is that we will allow our differences to pull us apart while we neglect the compelling ideas that bring us together. One of the most important of these ideas is that each of us has the right to speak and march and fight in defense of our liberty.

Campaign finance "reformers" today are endangering that liberty by giving government the right to create a so-called "level playing field" by restricting political speech. There are countries in the world whose governments already enjoy such power. Their names are Iraq, China and North Korea.

These same self-styled reformers are busy demonizing "special interests" in American politics. We are all special interests. Common Cause is a special interest. *The Washington Post* is a special interest. Harriet Beecher Stowe and the abolitionists who joined her call for the end of slavery were a special interest.

For that matter, Tom Paine was the "special interest" who helped start it all. Of course he didn't have to file with an FEC, but if they had been around back then, the reformers would have certainly tried to get their hands on him. In his famous pamphlet, Paine called for an "independence manifesto"—a call that resulted in the Declaration of Independence just eleven months later. Not bad, for "express advocacy."

# Censorship Does Not Threaten Freedom of the Press

## by William Powers

**About the author:** *William Powers was the media critic for the* New Republic *magazine before quitting in 1997.*

It's a curious but not entirely surprising fact that, in the age of media profusion, we dream of media repression. I'm speaking of the Censorship Fantasy, which varies in detail but always features the same general plot line: (1) you are living under a wicked regime that maintains power by censoring the truth; (2) you are one of the enlightened few who see through the appalling lies and cover-ups; (3) it is your mission to defeat the censors and thereby save civilization, which you will do, though it most likely will cost you your life.

## An Example of "Censorship"

The Censorship Fantasy is common today—many participants in talk radio suffer from it to an almost terminal degree—but very few of us get to live it out in reality, to feel the jackboot actually coming down on our keyboards. So I was naturally tickled and proud to learn that *The New Republic* had been censored. The news comes to us from Project Censored, an organization based at Sonoma State University in California, which issues an annual list of "the year's top 25 censored news stories." The winners for 1996 are out, and a *New Republic* piece came in third—the bronze medal of censorship! Who said it couldn't happen here?

Yet there are some strange aspects to this honor that I'm still puzzling over. One is that the censored piece, a column written by my colleague John B. Judis—who seems, when I see him around the office, to be totally unaware that he is just one step away from the gulag—has been published in full in Project Censored's new book, *Censored 1997*. When I learned from press reports of John's odd censored-yet-anthologized status—the annual announcement of the list of censored stories is a genuine media event, a wire-tingling, Nexis-spamming phenomenon—I figured the book might be difficult to obtain, perhaps only available in samizdat or through a post office box in Amsterdam. I wrote the title on a piece of paper, folded it several times and slipped quietly across the street, into a smallish bookstore of decidedly mainstream tastes. I checked the aisles for government agents, unfolded the paper and pushed it across the desk to the clerk, while I searched his eyes for glints of underground sympathy. "Uh, let's see," he said in a carelessly loud

> *"The term [censorship] has been . . . appropriated . . . to serve a political agenda."*

voice, as he clicked a few keys. "Yep. Says we should have two copies." He produced the book, not from the back room but from an open shelf near the front of the store; the audacity nearly took my breath away. It was an attractive paperback with blurbs on page two from Ralph Nader, the *Los Angeles Times* ("required reading") and many others. I hurriedly bought the volume and spirited it back to the office, where I closed the door and sat down to read the Judis piece, by flashlight.

It was a tight, characteristically well-reported number, revealing that the fine print in 1996's minimum-wage bill gave millions in unpublicized handouts to corporate America. Judis reports that these are typical of the "outrages" perpetrated by the 104th Congress, and that "they more than negate whatever good the bill may do." Pretty shocking stuff, and I was beginning to see why the censors had come down on the piece. But, when I got to the end, I started feeling a bit of déjà vu. It was as if I had read the censored piece before, even though I wasn't working at the magazine when Judis wrote it, before the clampdown got him. I turned to the front of the book, where the mystery was resolved. The censored piece, it turned out, had been published—in the October 28, 1996, issue of *The New Republic* and then put out over the United Media syndicate to newspapers around the country. A California daily called the *Santa Rosa Press Democrat* reprinted it, and that's apparently how it came to the attention of Project Censored.

## An Expansive Definition of Censorship

This, it seems, is "censorship," American style. It turns out that Project Censored, which has been at this for twenty years, uses what you might call an expansive definition of censorship. In fact, the rules say that for a story to be considered for the list, it must have "been published, either electronically or in print, in a circulated newspaper, journal, magazine, newsletter or similar publication. . . ." Project Censored director Peter Phillips writes: "We annually select and publish the most important under-covered news stories from hundreds of nominations. In today's corporate merger/takeover climate, our activities are essential to the continued vitality of the First Amendment."

*Chapter 1*

So now censorship is synonymous with "undercovered"? Something pernicious and deceptive is happening here, a change in the meaning of a vital and ancient concept: the suppression of ideas by the state. The original censors were two magistrates in ancient Rome, government officials who oversaw not only the census but public morals. And, in modern times, the term has been understood primarily to mean government silencing of writers, news organizations and artists. That is, at least until recently, when it was appropriated by groups like Project Censored to serve a political agenda.

Though the organization's board of "national judges" has included conservative TV host John McLaughlin, each year it is dominated by people associated with another worldview, the one which holds that the U.S. is now in the grip of a cartel of scary clerics, corporate plutocrats, white men in white hoods and gun-loving, misogynist tree-murderers. Some of 1997's judges have special expertise in censorship, such as the syndicated newspaper columnist and Pacifica Radio host Julianne Malveaux, who has written in favor of speech codes that would prohibit "the hurling of slurs in public space."

## Shouting Censorship

What this group targets is not real censorship of the sort experienced every day in China, Iran and Indonesia. It opposes the workings of the information market and the decisions that market reaches about what is news. Though the system is utterly free and open, it is true that some news organizations wield more power than others. The most powerful, which are to the right of the left and the left of the right, are very choosy about what they decide to call news. And those whose views are not selected for widest distribution would rather not think of themselves as losers in the game. So they shout censorship.

This is not to say that the mainstream press doesn't make mistakes. It makes many, some of them huge. But to call this censorship is to dilute the meaning of one of the most powerful words in the language—the word that we use to define our most basic freedom, the freedom to use other words. For anyone not captive to the pieties of the left or the right—and most people are too smart for either—the power and limitations of the mainstream are perfectly obvious. Those who want a hard-left point of view on current affairs know they are not going to get it from Judy Woodruff; so they tune in to Pacifica, pick up *Mother Jones*, read Molly Ivins or click on to the web site of *CovertAction Quarterly*. And for those who prefer to hear from the right, which promotes an equally silly

> *"To call [mistakes of the press] censorship is to dilute the meaning of one of the most powerful words in the language."*

conspiracist take on America (a nation in the thrall of the P.C. academics, ghastly feminists and depraved movie stars), relief is only as far away as Rush Limbaugh, *The American Spectator* and the Western Journalism Center's web site.

I visited the latter, on a tip that the Project Censored list has a mirror image at the other end of the spectrum, a twin so close in appearance, tone and even substance that one can glimpse the point where the fringes meet and merge. And there it was, "Operation Spike"—the WJC's annual list of "the biggest media cover-ups of the year" and "the most under-reported" stories. Though this list doesn't literally claim censorship, it suggests as much: in journalese, to "spike" a story is to kill it. I scrolled down through the short list of 1996 honorees, and soon found what I had fondly hoped and somehow knew would be there: a "spiked" *New Republic* story. It was a piece by Michael Fumento, arguing that then–Transportation Secretary Federico Peña was to blame for the infamous ValuJet crash, because he had allowed the airline to keep flying despite a terrible safety record. The WJC's problem with this story isn't really that it was "spiked," because of course it wasn't. It appeared in *The New Republic* on October 7, 1996—conspiratorially enough, just two weeks before the censored Judis column. The problem is that the article didn't bring the results conservatives wish it had. "Rather than fire Peña," the WJC fumes, "President Clinton named him his new Secretary of Energy, where he will be responsible for, among other things, monitoring the safety of the nation's nuclear reactors."

I walked down the hall of this, the most censored magazine in America, to dig through *The New Republic*'s archives for the issue with Fumento's piece so I could read it for myself. There were less than two dozen copies left on the shelf. It would be thrilling to think that on a dark night in October 1996 an unmarked government truck pulled up to our building and removed all the other copies, along with every last trace of that censored Judis piece. But it didn't happen that way. The magazines were gone for another reason: we sold them.

# The Extent of Book Banning Is Exaggerated

## by Steve McKinzie

**About the author:** *Steve McKinzie is the chair librarian at Dickinson College in Carlisle, Pennsylvania.*

This week (September 21st–27th, 1997), the nation celebrates National Banned Book Week, a week-long propaganda fest and consciousness-raising extravaganza of the American Library Association's Office for Intellectual Freedom. The week's promoters parade a list of books that they charge have been banned in libraries and schools across the nation, talk about the importance of First Amendment Rights, and lament the rise of censorship from what they consider to be the ill-informed and malicious enemies of freedom and American democracy—a group that includes the usual conservatives of various flavors and, of course, that enemy of everything dear to the national consciousness, the Christian Right.

### The ALA's Dishonesty

Now to begin with, most Americans have serious problems with the sort of radical libertarianism that the American Library Association (ALA) espouses. Most Americans don't buy into the notion that public libraries should buy anything, no matter how pornographic, or that schools should teach anything, no matter how controversial. The majority of Americans believe in community standards, and they stubbornly insist that schools, libraries, and other social institutions ought to support those standards. Even so, the real difficulty with the American Library Association's Banned Book Week isn't its philosophy, however much people may question the ALA's anything-goes-approach to building a library collection and managing a school's curriculum.

No, the real problem is the dishonesty involved.

Banned Book Week isn't really what it says it is. The ALA has gone in for some serious mislabeling here. It has misleadingly categorized the week—a se-

Reprinted from Steve McKinzie, "Banned Books Week 1997: A Case of Misrepresentation," *Covenant Syndicate*, vol. 1, no. 49, at http://capo.org/opeds/banbook.html, by permission of the author.

rious charge when you remember that librarians are supposed to be dispassionate and accurate catalogers or labelers of things.

In all honesty, what is the real state of censorship and book banning in America? Well, very few—if any—books in this country are currently banned. You can buy almost any title that you want, download tons of information from the Web that you need, and you can check out all sorts of things at your public library. Nor is censorship dangerously on the rise as the ALA is apt to insinuate.

## Exaggerated Notions of Censorship

The disparity between what actually is and what the week's promoters claim stems from their exaggerated notions of what constitutes censorship. In the eyes of the ALA and its Office for Intellectual Freedom, any kind of challenge to a book is to be considered an effort at banning and any kind of complaint about a title an attempt at unconscionable censorship. For a book to be labeled a banned book in their mind, someone needs only question its place in a given library's collection, or openly wonder if a specific title belongs in the children's section. To be reckoned a censor, one has only to suggest in public that a book may not be appropriate in a given high school English class.

*"Very few—if any—books in this country are currently banned."*

Kathy Monteiro, a teacher in McClintock High School in Tempe, Arizona, complained about her high schoolers' mandatory reading of *Huckleberry Finn*. She thought the book was racist. Parents in High Point, North Carolina, questioned the appropriateness of Richard Wright's *Native Son* and Alice Walker's *The Color Purple*. They thought the adult themes inappropriate for the grade level. Both these protests were officially recorded as examples of attempted censorship by ALA's *Newsletter on Intellectual Freedom*. All three titles were placed on the Banned Book List.

## The Right to Speak Out

Let's get real. Such challenges are not attempts at censorship, and such complaints about books used in a classroom are not efforts to have certain titles banned. The people involved in these controversies about what students are required to read are merely speaking their minds, and no matter how much I disagree with their contentions (I enjoy anything by Mark Twain and think Richard Wright's *Native Son* to be something of a classic), they have a right to argue their point. They should be able to speak up without fear of being considered enemies of the Republic or being chastised as censors of great literature.

Parents who challenge the inclusion of a given text in a specific literature class and citizens who openly protest a library's collection development decision are only speaking out about things that they believe in. It is a grand American tradition and one that we should encourage as much as we can. We shouldn't be trying to ban free speech in the name of free speech. Let people speak out about what they care about, without being branded a censor or labeled a book banner.

In short, the American Library Association needs to lighten up. At the very least, they should rename their week. As anyone can see, Banned Book Week isn't really about banned books. It is about people having differing opinions and caring enough to make those opinions known.

The nation could use a lot more of that, not less.

# Regulations on Harassing Speech Do Not Threaten Free Speech on College Campuses

by Thomas C. Grey

**About the author:** *Thomas C. Grey is Sweitzer Professor of Law at Stanford Law School.*

Slogans have their place. I have put bumper stickers on my car from time to time, recognizing that they can't treat the full complexity of an issue. But sometimes it is important to make things simple, and a good slogan can do that. "No Speech Codes" is a particularly persuasive slogan. Alan Kors is colorful in uttering it and just as persuasive when he gives his Voltairian advice on how to deal with any campus speech code: "Crush this infamy!"

That got him a lot of amens. And how could any believer in intellectual freedom at the university be for a campus speech code? I never thought of myself as a proponent of "speech codes." Only after I drafted a campus regulation at Stanford did I discover that apparently I had written one. And not surprisingly, once it was seen in that light, once that label was affixed to it, it was a dead duck. A state court recently struck it down.

I'd like to ask you to think a little bit further about the slogan "No Speech Codes," and how its very effective rhetorical force worked out in this case. I don't suppose any of you will say amen to what I have to say, but maybe I can get some of you to see a problem here that is not a matter for slogans or amens on either side.

I'm going to take it as given that there is a legitimate case for universities prohibiting harassment of students on discriminatory grounds, grounds of race or sex. The case is roughly the same as the case for making harassment based on sex and race illegal in the workplace. Some might debate the premise, but I'm addressing myself to those of you who accept it.

## Defining Harassing Speech

The problem then is that harassment can be carried out by means of speech. So if you are going to prohibit harassment, you are going to regulate speech, and when you do that you create the danger of suppressing debate, suppressing ideas. My idea is that when that danger arises, we are better off making clear and defining in objective terms what speech can be regulated, what speech can count as harassment.

The alternative, which Alan Kors recommended, is simply to prohibit harassment and leave it to case-by-case determination what conduct shall fall under the prohibition. That's what

> *"If you are going to prohibit harassment, you are going to regulate speech."*

the slogan "No Speech Codes" leads to—you can't specify in advance what kind of speech may count as harassment, can't specify it by content, because if you do that, you have written a speech code.

A number of courts in campus speech cases have gone the route suggested by the slogan. In trying to protect free debate on campus, they have not looked directly for intolerance of controversial ideas, but rather have used as a proxy for ideological intolerance a university's mention of the content of speech in its harassment regulation. Our own case at Stanford is the clearest example of this.

But the kind of regulation that specifies what kind of speech counts as harassment is more protective of speech, in my opinion, than is an open-ended ban on harassment that leaves what speech falls under its ban to case-by-case determination. And yet no one is arguing that these open-ended antiharassment rules violate the First Amendment. My school, having been disabled by the courts from defining harassing speech—because to do so is to institute a speech code—is now back to the position of having one of these open-ended bans, and no one is complaining that academic freedom or intellectual freedom is under siege.

So in both debates, the cultural debates on campuses and the legal debates in the courts, the slogan "No Speech Codes" has triumphed. The basic idea behind the slogan is right—that intellectual freedom should be vigorously protected, and that this protection requires adhering to some firm principles. But the slogan, and the associated principle of no content regulation of speech, has in my opinion been less friendly toward free debate on campus than is the alternate principle that regulations touching speech must be clear, objective, and narrowly drawn, rather than vague and open-ended.

## Reconciling Policies

Now let me come to cases, or rather my particular case, the Stanford case. Stanford's regulation was an attempt to reconcile two existing university policies: first, our prohibition against discrimination in provision of educational services on racial and other invidious grounds; and second, our guarantee of free speech and free debate on campus. Both of these principles had been articulated and implemented in concrete ways in the recent past—in the case of speech, for example, by prohibiting disruption of campus speeches, a regulation dating from the troubles of the 1970s.

In the case of our antidiscrimination principle, a concrete issue that arose in recent years was harassment. It is clear as a matter of federal law as well as of common sense that one way of discriminating against students in the provision of educational services is to stand by and do nothing while students are harassed on the basis of their race and sex while they are trying to study, go to class, and get their work done. This is now as well-recognized a form of discrimination as denying admission to people or refusing to graduate them or giving them lower grades on the basis of race or sex.

On the other hand, on a university campus as distinguished from an ordinary workplace, if you just prohibit discriminatory harassment without further definition you get yourself into the problem that many of you are aware of and rightly exercised about—the problem that the expression of unpopular ideas can be enmeshed in campus disciplinary processes. If you say something that offends a group, or a cause or an ideology, those who strongly disagree can complain about having to listen to ideas they find offensive. And then if you keep on saying what you know offends people, you can be charged with harassing them by doing so. The excuse of harassment can thereby be used as a way of silencing unpopular views.

## The Three Elements of Stanford's Regulation

Faced with this dilemma, we at Stanford thought it best to define in a narrow and specific way what kind of speech could count as harassment, rather than leave the matter to case-by-case determination with the accompanying chilling effect of uncertainty. Our definition had three elements.

First, to count as harassment speech had to contain a racial epithet, or an equivalent expression referring to sex, sexual preference, national origin, or religion. We defined this as a word or other symbol that was "commonly understood" to convey hatred or contempt for the group in question. The idea behind "commonly understood" was to ensure that groups could not by themselves define what terms would count as epithets—a term had

> *"One way of discriminating against students . . . is to stand by and do nothing while students are harassed on the basis of their race and sex."*

to be understood generally across the society as having this force. We all know these epithets, and if we don't know them as such, they don't meet the test of being "commonly understood." So to count as harassment, speech had to contain one of these words, or an equivalent nonverbal symbol, like a swastika or a burning cross.

Second, and this is very important, to count as harassment the speech had to be directly addressed to an individual to whom the epithet was applied. This completely immunized all public address, speech, writing, and the like on campus. You can carry a placard, you can make a public speech, you can print a pamphlet, you can put something in the student newspaper that uses racial epithets in the most offensive way and you still don't violate the regulation. Harassment is private hassling, not public discourse.

> *"You can put something in the student newspaper that uses racial epithets in the most offensive way and you still don't violate the [Stanford speech] regulation."*

Third, the term has to be used with intent to insult the person addressed. This is meant to deal with the situation where someone uses an epithet to someone, thinking it is okay to do so in jest, or because the speaker has heard members of the group use the epithet among themselves. That might be insensitive, but it wouldn't count as harassment because it was not intended to hurt or insult.

## A Workable Regulation Struck Down

We thus defined, admittedly in somewhat legalistic fashion, the kind of speech that could count as harassment. If speech met these three conditions, it was harassment, otherwise it was not. Having defined harassment by speech in these narrow and specific terms, in order to avoid the vagueness and chilling effect of an open-ended ban on harassment, we were said to have written a speech code. And that is basically what did us in. Our regulation was attacked by many civil libertarians as an impermissible content regulation of speech on campus, which is the lawyer's way of saying "Speech Code!" Some civil liberties people did think we had found a reasonable way of dealing with the conflict between free speech and antidiscrimination that arises in the context of harassment. But most ended up buying the "No Speech Codes" slogan, and finally our rule was indeed struck down by the courts.

That came about as a result of a California statute that applied First Amendment standards to private schools and universities. I should say, parenthetically, that I think that statute was a bad idea. I agree with Alan Kors on that point, mainly because I think that people should be free to set up ideologically sectarian private colleges, just as they are free to set up religiously sectarian ones. Then people can go to these colleges, knowing that they ban the expression of ideas at odds with their fundamental commitments—why shouldn't this be allowed?

But that's not my point here. I'm not defending Stanford on the ground of the right of private institutions to have ideological commitments that they enforce through speech regulations. Stanford doesn't purport to be that kind of institution; it is rather a general university open to all ideas. I think the Stanford regulation should have been upheld, but I think the same regulation should be upheld at a public university as well. A number of public universities have regulations roughly like Stanford's, including the University of California system, and the University of Texas, and I hope those regulations will be upheld—I think they should be.

I don't necessarily think every university should adopt Stanford's kind of regulation. It seems to me very much a local matter whether the situation, the history, the conditions of the place make it appropriate to have this kind of regime. But it seems to me that these narrow rules should be accepted as legal, and then it should be debated at the local level whether in policy terms they are right for the place in question.

## An Erroneous Ruling

As a matter of technical constitutional law, I do think the invalidation of the Stanford provision was wrong. Nadine Strossen and I can debate this later if you like, but I don't think you are primarily interested in the details of First Amendment law. I'll say only briefly why I think the court's decision involved a misreading of the Supreme Court's decision in *RAV v. City of St. Paul.*

The *RAV* decision struck down an ordinance that made it a crime to utter racially inflammatory and other group-based fighting words. The Court said that governments could prohibit all fighting words, but could not discriminate in speech regulation against group-based fighting words.

But the Court created an important exception for general regulations of discriminatory conduct, like the prohibition of discrimination in employment in Title VII of the Civil Rights Act of 1964. Governments can prohibit discriminatory conduct, and can sweep up discriminatory speech that is included in the relevant category of conduct. If you prohibit discriminatory conduct in employment, and if one form of discriminatory conduct is harassment, and if harassment can be carried out through speech, the fact that harassing speech that is discriminatory gets prohibited as part of the general prohibition of discriminatory conduct does not violate the principle of *RAV*. The Supreme Court was unanimous on that point.

> *"Discriminatory conduct includes discriminatory harassment. Speech can harass."*

But that was exactly what Stanford was doing. We had a general regulation that prohibited discriminatory conduct on campus. Discriminatory conduct includes discriminatory harassment. Speech can harass. But if the speech that can count as harassment is not carefully defined, free debate can be chilled by a prohibition of discriminatory harassment. We took care narrowly and specifically to define the speech that could count as harassment. So when the local state court struck our regulation down, it failed to take account of the important exception the Court had made in *RAV*.

But I don't mean to debate the legal question here. What you are interested in is the policy question. The basic policy point is that the Stanford way of doing it is more speech-protective than the alternative. The alternative is what we are back to now.

## Prohibit Harassment, Not "Speech"

Once the Stanford rule is struck down, what does the university do? As a lawyer, I would take account of the climate that has been created in the courts and the larger society by the success of the slogan "No Speech Codes." I would advise campus administrators to drop all references to speech in their regulations. Don't mention speech. That is what triggers the invocation of this most effective slogan.

Of course you have to prohibit discrimination, both as a matter of basic morality and as a requirement of federal law. And discriminatory harassment is universally understood as a form of improper discrimination, both in law and more generally as a matter of social morality. But of course discriminatory harassment is just a subset of harassment generally. So to avoid all appearance of ideological partisanship, the prudent thing to do is just to prohibit harassment generally. And that is what Stanford has now done, in the wake of the court decision invalidating the narrower regulation I drafted.

> *"I would advise campus administrators to drop all references to speech in their regulations. Don't mention speech."*

What does harassment include? The kind of conduct that has most readily been recognized as requiring prohibition as unlawful harassment over the last couple of decades is stalking. This is a general problem in society, and a problem on university campuses. Someone gets romantically obsessed with someone else who does not reciprocate, and starts following the person around, makes phone calls, leaves notes that may or may not have an explicitly threatening character—and yet the overall course of conduct is certainly threatening, experienced as threatening by the victim, and reasonably so. In that situation, the law steps in and says "you can't do that, you can't do that kind of thing." Unfortunately it is a little hard to define in precise terms what "that kind of thing" is, but on the other hand there is widespread agreement that core cases of stalking are a problem that is appropriately addressed by the law and prohibited. This is so even though much of the conduct that constitutes stalking—phone calls, notes, approaches on the street—involves speech. Most people agree that it is not a violation of values of free expression to punish this kind of speech when it is part of a course of conduct that amounts to harassment.

Now let us bring that prohibition to the campus and see what might be done with it if the overlap of harassment with speech and debate is not addressed explicitly. Let me try a hypothetical case on you. Suppose an African-American undergraduate at a major university protests that a number of white students in his dormitory are going out of their way to talk about *The Bell Curve* in his hearing, expressing their admiration for its methods, its findings, and its thesis. He has made clear that he doesn't want to hear this, that it is offensive to him, but they keep on talking about it so that he can hear. He regards this as an assault on his beliefs and on himself, and he considers it harassment.

A controversy blows up on campus over this episode—not too hypothetical, right? The campus newspaper interviews the white students and they say that they indeed agree with *The Bell Curve*, accept its critique of affirmative action, and think it means that the complaining student doesn't really belong at the university. If he doesn't like what they are saying, and he leaves as a consequence of having to hear it, that is fine with them.

That could lead to the white students' being charged with harassment of the African-American student, could it not? There is at least a plausible case. They have admitted that they know they are annoying him, and it could be concluded that they are doing so with intent to drive him out. In colloquial terms, they could be said to be harassing him. And under a campus regulation that simply prohibited "harassment," without further definition of what that means when the harassment is carried on by means of speech, such a charge would not be obviously invalid.

By contrast, under the former Stanford regulation it would be clear there was no actionable harassment here. No racial epithet had been used; that would be the end of the matter as a disciplinary case. Incidentally, the rule would have equally readily put an end to any attempt to discipline the white student at Pennsylvania who used the term "water buffalo" in reference to black students. This, too, is not a commonly recognized racial epithet, and that would have been the end of the case.

So that's the basic thrust of my argument to you. The old Stanford rule clearly protected these politically incorrect conservative students against campus discipline for their unpopular speech. Now that we are back to a general prohibition of harassment, things are not so clear. That is the famous victory that was won by the application of the very effective slogan "No Speech Codes."

I would just ask you to think again about that slogan before you next apply it. It has clearly appropriate applications. There are many explicit speech regulations on campuses that should be struck down by courts, and there are many more that should be gotten rid of by internal processes. But there are also explicit and content-based regulations of speech that are appropriate to protect students against discriminatory harassment, and that are better than vague prohibitions of "harassment" at protecting the right to free expression of unpopular ideas.

# A Flag-Burning Amendment Would Protect Free Speech

by Richard Parker

**About the author:** *Richard Parker is a professor of constitutional law at Harvard University.*

Supporting the flag amendment is a way of supporting freedom of speech. Does that surprise you? If you followed only the media's coverage of the issue, it would. For the media—like most opponents of the amendment—insist on framing the question as "protecting the flag versus protecting free speech." This is a clever move. But it is a misleading, cynical maneuver. It is time to set things straight.

I want to make five points. Because our opponents have distorted the issue, I'll start by countering their most negative arguments. Then I'll make the case for the amendment as a much-needed enhancement of freedom of speech.

## Amending a Mistake

We're often told the flag amendment would "amend the First Amendment." This is nonsense. All it would "amend" is a recent mistake by the Supreme Court.

For more than 200 years, constitutional lawyers—beginning with James Madison, the "father" of the First Amendment—believed that the people, through their government, could protect their flag from desecration. The people exercised the power. No one supposed it abridged the freedom of speech. In our own era, great champions of free speech endorsed the practice. One was Justice Hugo Black, the leader in developing modern First-Amendment law. Another was Chief Justice Earl Warren. The practice and endorsement of flag protection is, therefore, both deeply rooted and of very long standing in our constitutional tradition.

The disruption came only in 1989. That was when a narrow majority of the justices, by a 5-4 vote, suddenly decided to "read" the First Amendment as for-

Reprinted from Richard Parker, "The Mirage of Slippery Slopes," *The American Legion Magazine*, July 1998, by permission of the author.

bidding specific protection of the American flag. This decision would be surgically removed by the proposed amendment.

The First Amendment itself will, of course, remain wholly intact; it will simply have restored to it the meaning long taken completely for granted.

## Fear of a Slippery Slope Is Exaggerated

Opponents of the flag amendment, nonetheless, are addicted to exaggeration. In alarm, they go on to insist it would open the door to imprisonment of individuals who paint pictures or wear clothing or advertise businesses with an image of the flag. Even worse, they say, it would start us down a slippery slope, "amending away" all of our freedom of speech, step by step. This is absurd.

The amendment, in fact, is very limited. All it would do is permit Congress (not the states) to protect an actual "flag" (not an image of a flag) from physical desecration— burning it, urinating on it, defecating on it. Congress would be allowed to prohibit such acts, but the amendment does not specify imprisonment.

> *"For more than 200 years, constitutional lawyers . . . believed that the people, through their government, could protect their flag from desecration."*

Its carefully focused language is answer enough to the pretended fears of its potential application.

Basic constitutional safeguards give the lie, moreover, to panic over a "slippery slope." Whatever law Congress enacts must win the support of both houses. It is subject to presidential veto. Judges and juries oversee the case-by-case enforcement of any law. And if others were to go on and promote other, broader constitutional amendments, they'd face the process of ratification. More than 11,000 amendments have been proposed. Only 27 have been ratified. If there's a slope, it runs uphill.

Although you might not know it from the scare rhetoric typical of our opponents, the United States should not be confused with Nazi Germany or the Soviet Union.

## Squelching No Viewpoint

This confusion is, in fact, the crux of the court's mistake. Its 1989 decision turned on a claim that, in singling out our national symbol for protection, government was discriminating in favor of one "point of view"—and against competing "points of view." Discrimination among competing views does, indeed, violate a basic First Amendment principle. But the justices misapplied the principle. For the American flag, unlike some others, does not represent just one "point of view." It does not stand for one party or one government. It is, as the dissenting justices insisted, "unique." It stands for our nation, for what we have in common, above our differences.

By authorizing the flag's protection, the proposed amendment, therefore, would squelch no viewpoint. Those wanting to express any message would be free to do so by any means other than trashing a flag. A minimal respect for our national community—as symbolized by the American flag—would simply be recognized as separate from contention among diverse points of view.

## The Amendment Enhances Freedom of Speech

Opponents of the flag amendment try to trivialize it, claiming it's meant to protect the feelings of a minority of hypersensitive people. (Patriots are the ones they have in mind.) This, they say, undermines free speech. But they miss the point. For the aim of the amendment is not to protect anyone's "feelings," but to enhance—at its very foundation—the freedom of speech.

A robust system of free speech—of wide-open disagreement with one another—depends, at bottom, on connection to one another. It depends on community. It depends on some agreement that, despite our differences, we are *one*, that the problem of any American is *our* problem. Without this much connection, why listen to one another? Why not just see who can yell louder and who is stronger? Civil-rights leaders understood the danger. They saw the importance, especially to minorities appealing to majorities, of respect for the value—and the unique symbol—of national community. That is why they displayed the American flag so proudly in the great marches of the 1960s.

Respect for this value—and so the foundation of free speech—has eroded. Special-interest groups and elitists of all sorts celebrate not connection but separatism. They might say smugly they love the flag. But they instruct us that the flag stands, now, for the freedom to desecrate it. Where will this leave a Martin Luther King Jr. of tomorrow?

The number of incidents of flag desecration, about 60 in the last four years, is not the heart of the matter. What matters most is our response to them. The key response has been that of the court. By degrading our symbol of national community to a "point of view" in competition with that of a flag burner, by doing so in the name of the First Amendment, the five justices did real damage to opportunity for effective exercise of rights under that amendment. To undo the damage we have one recourse. That is to exercise our right under *Article V* of the Constitution.

> *"The aim of the [flag] amendment is . . . to enhance— at its very foundation—the freedom of speech."*

## Testing Our Freedom

Exercising the right to amend the Constitution is participation in—and a test of—our system of freedom of speech. Because it's an uphill struggle, it calls for commitment to the possibility of open debate. Yet, because it threatens elite control over the Constitution, it calls up, in opposition, the most repressive instincts. Opponents of the flag amendment wrap themselves in the mantle of free speech, but they routinely mock it. Robotically, they repeat the same so-called arguments, irresponsibly trivializing and exaggerating the effect of the proposed amendment, blankly ignoring the case for it.

This is the test of our own faith in the freedom of speech. This is our chance to show that, while our opponents are afraid of open debate, while they try to shut it down, we will make clear to all that it is we, not they, who are the true supporters of the First Amendment.

# Limits on Campaign Spending Do Not Threaten Free Speech

## by Bob Schiff

**About the author:** *Bob Schiff is a staff attorney at the Congress Watch division of Public Citizen, a consumer advocacy organization.*

Campaign-finance scandals dominate the headlines. Public sentiment for reform is at its highest level since the Watergate era. Yet it seems like the opposition to reform in 1997 was bolder, and the odds are getting longer. Even the McCain-Feingold bill, which many reformers characterize as only a weak first step, faces heated and determined opposition. [The McCain-Feingold bill was defeated in March 1998.] Free marketeers aligned with the American Civil Liberties Union (ACLU) and the Christian Right denounce attempts to reform the loophole-ridden, corruption-breeding system we now live with as attacks on the sacred right of free speech.

It is no longer laughable in Congress to talk about getting rid of all limits on campaign contributions. "The reforms enacted after Watergate failed," critics say. "Let's just get rid of all restrictions, disclose everything, and let the public decide." That such a proposal gets a respectful hearing in Congress and on the editorial pages of major dailies shows how far the debate has moved.

Now, more than ever, progressives need to make federal campaign-finance reform a priority. And while it is important to keep long-term goals in mind, incremental solutions may offer our best chance to make progress toward more sweeping change. Giving up altogether is simply not an option, unless we don't care that the public thinks Congress is up for auction, that voter turnout is at an all-time low, and that corporate money drowns out the voices of average people both in the legislature and on the campaign trail.

The simple reason why we need campaign-finance reform is that money influences policy.

Reprinted from Bob Schiff, "The ACLU vs. Public Citizen: A Debate on Campaign Finance Reform," pro view: "The First Amendment Is Not a Stop Sign Against Reform," *The Progressive*, December 1997, by permission of *The Progressive*, 409 E. Main St., Madison, WI 53703.

The players are different, the legislative issues come and go. But the one constant in our political system is the need for money. Lots of it. Candidate and party spending in the 1996 elections topped $2 billion. Hundreds of millions more were spent in unreported "issue ads." The constant search for funding to run campaigns costs us dearly. Candidates and elected officials spend inordinate amounts of time raising money, and the pressure to cross the line into improper or even illegal activity can test the resolve of even the most ethical politicians.

> *"Free marketeers . . . denounce attempts to reform the loophole-ridden, corruption-breeding system . . . as attacks on the sacred right of free speech."*

It would be one thing if the people with big money to spend on elections were merely civic-minded or disinterested rich people, or even just wealthy ideologues from across the political spectrum, but they're not. Nor does a broad cross-section of the public make political contributions. Less than one-third of 1 percent of the population gave contributions totaling more than $200 in the 1996 election. A huge proportion of the campaign cash that politicians raise comes from business interests, giving them special access to and influence over the legislative process.

Take two major policy debates of the last two Congresses: health care and the new telecommunications law.

## Money and Health-Care Reform

Remember the Clinton plan? Thirty-seven million Americans with no insurance? Harry and Louise? The Democrats squabbled, the Republicans obstructed, and the legislation imploded.

During the ill-fated health-care debate, campaign money flowed freely from those with an economic interest in shaping the legislation. According to the Center for Responsive Politics, individuals and PACs [political action committees] associated with the health industry (including doctors, hospitals, nursing homes, HMOs [health maintenance organizations], and drug companies) made more than $37 million in contributions to candidates, split evenly between Democrats and Republicans. The American Medical Association alone contributed more than $2.5 million. At least sixty members of Congress who sat on one of the five committees with jurisdiction over the health-care legislation received more than $50,000 in contributions from these health-industry PACs and individuals.

In the end, opponents of reform won. Today, the number of uninsured Americans is more than forty million, and the corporatization of our health-care system continues unabated.

## Telecommunications Policy

Fast-forward to the next Congress. The Republicans are in control and undertaking a massive rewrite of the telecommunications laws. A titanic struggle ensues among the Baby Bells, the long-distance phone companies, and the cable TV companies that want to compete for each other's business. The money flows again: According to the Center for Responsive Politics, in the 1996 election cycle the cable companies contributed more than $2 million to candidates and parties, the long-distance companies gave nearly $4 million, and the Baby Bells coughed up an astonishing $6.2 million.

As a result of that fight, consumers found themselves out in the cold. Cable rates went up, and the networks got an enormous government giveaway: The whole digital television spectrum is now theirs for free.

## Tax Breaks and Giveaways

It is not just the colossal struggles of big-money interests on major legislative issues that show the need for reform. Tax loopholes and corporate-welfare giveaways manage to find their way into legislation with little or no public discussion.

We're all now familiar with the $50 billion tax break that Senate Majority Leader Trent Lott, Republican of Mississippi, and House Speaker Newt Gingrich, Republican of Georgia, engineered for the tobacco companies. When that deal was exposed, the public outcry forced Congress to repeal it. Tobacco companies' soft-money contributions of $5.7 million to the Republican Party in 1996 and another $1.6 million in the first six months of 1997 surely greased the wheels for that effort to slip one by us.

> *"The simple reason why we need campaign-finance reform is that money influences policy."*

And how about the $280 million special tax break for Amway Corporation? Amway Chairman Richard De Vos and his wife contributed $1 million in soft money to the Republican party in 1997. That follows on the heels of the $315,000 that Amway gave to the Republicans in the 1996 cycle, and the $2.5 million—the biggest single contribution ever—the company contributed in 1994.

Maybe Amway would have gotten its tax break, and all major legislative fights would turn out exactly the same if the interested parties didn't make campaign contributions. Maybe. But I doubt it. One poll showed 86 percent of Americans believing that campaign contributions influence policy decisions— and that poll was taken before the current scandals. Public perception is important. It affects whether people trust the Congress to do the right thing. And it affects whether people feel it is worth participating in the political system on election day.

## Reform Does Not Violate the First Amendment

Opponents of campaign-finance reform, like Senator Mitch McConnell, Republican of Kentucky, love to wrap themselves in the Constitution. The ACLU is a willing accomplice. The 1976 Supreme Court decision in *Buckley v. Valeo*, which threw out limits on campaign expenditures by candidates, is their battle cry. They argue that every reform proposal aimed at reducing the domination of the political system by big money violates the First Amendment. "Money equals speech," they proclaim. "The First Amendment is not a loophole."

It isn't. But it's not an impenetrable roadblock to reform, either. There is nuance in this area of the law that the ACLU and Senator McConnell prefer to ignore.

The most important thing to remember when the First Amendment is held up like a stop sign against reform is that the *Buckley* decision *upheld* limits on campaign contributions. Candidates can spend as much as they want on their own campaigns, the Court held, but contributions from citizens should be limited. The Court reasoned that candidates have a right, as a matter of free expression, to spend their own money on their own campaigns. But campaign contributions can create corruption, or the appearance of corruption. So, in the interest of democratic government, they can be curbed. The Court therefore upheld limits on individual contributors of $1,000 per candidate per election. It also upheld a limit of $25,000 on the total annual contributions that individuals may make to candidates, parties, and PACs.

> *"The* **Buckley** *decision* **upheld** *limits on campaign contributions."*

The *Buckley* decision also upheld the system by which we have funded Presidential elections in this country since 1976 with taxpayer money. Simply put, it is constitutional to offer candidates a very tempting inducement—about $60 million in public funds for Presidential candidates in the last election—to limit their spending. The limits in the Presidential system are voluntary. Ross Perot and Steve Forbes decided not to abide by them.

These important components of the *Buckley* decision, which the ACLU argued against at the time and with which it still disagrees, mean that central provisions of the reform bill introduced by Senators John McCain, Republican of Arizona, and Russ Feingold, Democrat of Wisconsin, would be upheld by the Court. Those provisions—a ban on the unlimited corporate, labor union, and individual contributions to the political parties known as "soft money," and voluntary spending limits for Congressional campaigns, made more attractive by the offer of free and reduced-rate TV time for those who limit their spending—are worthy and constitutional goals. More far-reaching inducements to candidates to voluntarily limit their spending, like providing clean public money for all Congressional elections, would also pass constitutional muster.

## Issue Ads Should Be Regulated

Another difficult but not insurmountable problem is the growing use of phony issue ads to make an end-run around contribution limits and the prohibition on corporate contributions to federal elections. Most of the money the political parties raise goes to pay for TV ads. Television is the single greatest expense for most candidates. Candidates are often happy when their contributors channel money into "issue ads."

Thus we've seen the rise of ads that claim to be about important issues, but actually are thinly veiled campaign advertisements. In 1996, one ad accused a candidate of beating his wife. The ad didn't urge viewers to vote against the candidate, just to call him and "tell him we don't approve of his wrongful behavior." Citizens For Reform, the tax-exempt group founded by conservative activist Peter Flaherty that paid for the ad, spent $2 million in the two months before the election to air ads in fifteen Congressional districts. Triad Management, a Washington, D.C.–based political consulting firm run by a former fundraiser for Oliver North, helped steer wealthy donors to the group. At least one made a $100,000 contribution.

Candidates pay for such ads out of funds that are subject to the election laws; outside groups should, too. *Buckley* itself permits the regulation of ads that expressly advocate the election or defeat of candidates. And in a 1990 decision, *Austin v. Chamber of Commerce*, the Supreme Court recognized the power of the legislature to address "the corrosive and distorting effects of immense aggregations of wealth that are accumulated with the help of the corporate form and that have little or no correlation to the public's support for the corporation's political ideas."

> **"Buckley *itself permits the regulation of ads that expressly advocate the election or defeat of candidates."***

Congress should try to fine-tune the definition of "express advocacy," based on the real-life experience of the 1996 elections. Phony issue ads paid for by corporate funds should not dominate and distort the electoral debate.

Court decisions and FEC [Federal Election Commission] rulings, combined with the ingenuity of candidates and outside groups, have shredded the campaign-finance system passed by Congress in the wake of the Watergate scandal. By 1996, we had unlimited campaign spending and unlimited contributions again—only this time through the soft-money and phony issue-ad loophole. And we had more scandals.

## A Frightening Proposal

How do conservatives respond? By promoting a bill that would make the problem of money in politics even worse. Aptly named for its chief House sponsor, Representative John Doolittle, Republican of California, the bill would wipe out all limits on individual campaign contributions to candidates, PACs, and parties, while requiring all contributions to be disclosed on the Internet within twenty-four hours. The Cato Institute [a libertarian think tank] loves this idea: Adam Smith meets the FEC.

A system of unlimited contributions to candidates is frightening to contemplate. Major legislative battles already are cash cows for members of Congress.

Under the Doolittle bill, they will be gold mines. Just get on the right commit-tee, open your bank account, and watch the money stream in. The incentive for corporations to launder contributions through employees will be hard to resist and even harder to police. Why raise eyebrows by having twenty-five employ-ees, including some secretaries and clerks, send in $1,000 checks? Just funnel the $25,000 or even $100,000 to your favorite Senator through a wealthy executive.

> *"A system of unlimited contributions to candidates is frightening to contemplate."*

But won't disclosure solve all these problems? Here's the theory: Just give the public all the information, and if it thinks candidates are for sale to the wrong people, it won't elect them. Sounds good, but it won't work. We actually have a pretty good system of disclosure now. It's not instantaneous, but the information is available fairly quickly, espe-cially in the final month of the campaign. The problem is not disclosure but public access, public understanding, and timing. Not everyone has a computer. Not everyone with a computer has access to the Internet, or the technical capa-bility to obtain campaign-finance information and make sense of it.

Once very rich people can give unlimited amounts directly to candidates or PACs, voters will have an incredible burden added to their decision-making process. And not much information to go on. Even if a vigilant press does its best to help, it won't be enough. The information may also come too late. Polit-ical contributions flow throughout the election cycle, as legislation is being considered in Congress. For example, AT&T's PAC distributed $166,000 to federal candidates on a single day in late 1995, the day after a compromise on the telecommunications legislation was reached.

Imagine this scenario: The Doolittle bill is law. Early in 1998, an electric-utility executive gives $100,000 to the chairman of the Senate Energy Commit-tee, which is marking up the electricity deregulation bill the next week. The Senator, who was re-elected in 1996, drops a provision from the bill that would have prohibited utilities from passing on to consumers all of the costs from their failed nuclear plants. A year later, reeling from your swollen electricity bill, you get on your computer and trace the money, figure out the timing of the contribution and the legislation, and decide to act. Congratulations! You can vote against your Senator in 2002.

# Chapter 2

# Should There Be Limits to Free Speech?

# Chapter Preface

In January 1999, members of the Vietnamese-American community in the Little Saigon section of Los Angeles held protests outside the Hi-Tek Video Store. Demonstrators were outraged because the store's owner, Truong Van Tran, a Vietnamese immigrant, had hung a poster of Ho Chi Minh in his window, along with a North Vietnamese flag. To many Vietnamese Americans, these symbols were vivid reminders of the terror and violence inflicted on them and their families by Ho's regime during the Vietnam War, the trauma they experienced as refugees, and the ongoing repression of their homeland under communism. As one Little Saigon resident, Tony Truong, states, "For the communist flag to be displayed in Little Saigon is not just an insult to our community, it is a rusty nail through our hearts."

The protesters claimed that Tran's display of the communist symbols amounted to "fighting words"—a deliberate attempt to provoke conflict—and was therefore illegal. In response to the demonstrations, a restraining order was issued forcing Tran to remove the display. Superior Court Judge Tam Nomoto Schumann overturned the order, upholding Tran's right to hang the flag and poster. When Tran returned to his store, escorted by police, to re-hang the flag and poster, he was attacked by a crowd of angry protesters.

The incident in Little Saigon illustrates how the ideal of free speech, which seems so simple in theory, can quickly become controversial. In the abstract, few people would argue in favor of restricting people's freedom to express their views. But when those views hit close to home, restrictions on speech can seem like a reasonable response to uncivilized behavior. Thus many Americans favor restrictions on indecent entertainment and art, hate speech, or even speech that exposes children to ideas their parents do not want them exposed to.

Civil libertarians, on the other hand, insist that the best remedy for offensive speech is not censorship but open debate. While discussing hate speech, the American Civil Liberties Union (ACLU) states:

> Speech that deeply offends our morality or is hostile to our way of life warrants the same constitutional protection as other speech because the right of free speech is indivisible: When one of us is denied this right, all of us are denied. . . . Where racist, sexist and homophobic speech is concerned, the ACLU believes that more speech—not less—is the best revenge.

The debate over whether certain types of speech should be restricted is presented in the following chapter.

# Obscenity in Popular Culture Should Be Censored

## by Robert H. Bork, Interviewed by Michael Cromartie

**About the authors:** *Robert H. Bork is the John H. Olin Scholar in Legal Studies at the American Enterprise Institute, a conservative public policy research organization in Washington, D.C. He gained national recognition in 1987, when his nomination to the U.S. Supreme Court was rejected following a heated Senate debate. Michael Cromartie is an advisory editor for* Christianity Today *magazine.*

*Michael Cromartie: Your book* [Slouching Towards Gomorrah: Modern Liberalism and American Decline] *describes the role the Supreme Court has played in promoting cultural decline in America. How has that happened?*

*Robert H. Bork:* Consider *Cohen v. California* (1971), a case in which a young man wore a jacket into a courthouse that had obscenities written on the back that suggested performing an implausible sexual act with the Selective Service System. He was arrested, and the Supreme Court said he couldn't be convicted. One of the reasons given was "Who was to say what was obscene?" The majority opinion actually said, "One man's vulgarity is another man's lyric." If you want radical individualism and moral relativism, there you are.

*You write that "Sooner or later censorship is going to have to be considered as popular culture continues plunging to ever more sickening lows." Are you advocating censorship?*

Yes.

### Censorship Is Nothing New

*What fine distinctions do you make?*

I don't make any fine distinctions; I'm just advocating censorship. It's odd that we've grown so sensitive about the topic of censorship that if somebody

Excerpted from "Give Me Liberty, but Don't Give Me Filth," an interview with Robert H. Bork, by Michael Cromartie, *Christianity Today*, May 19, 1997. Reprinted by permission of Michael Cromartie.

mentions it everybody begins to shake all over and say, "Oh my! That's an unthinkable thought." We had censorship in this country up until the last couple of decades. Almost all of our national existence we had censorship. When I was practicing law in Chicago as a young lawyer, the city of Chicago had a censorship board for movies. It didn't suppress any good art, it didn't eliminate any ideas; but it did keep a certain amount of filth out of the theaters.

> *"We had censorship in this country up until the last couple of decades. Almost all of our national existence we had censorship."*

*How would this censorship actually work?*

We don't have to guess how censorship would work; we've seen it work. It's just like any other law. You get the elected representatives to write a code about what is obscene and can be prohibited, and then an executive branch official applies the code to some instance. If the person involved thinks the code has been misapplied, or that the code itself is defective, he goes to the courts for relief.

Unfortunately, the Supreme Court, in the service of radical individualism (I am talking about *Cohen v. California*), has set up three tests you have to get through to prosecute obscenity, and it's almost impossible to satisfy those three tests. The Court became very nervous about allowing any prohibition of offensive sexual acts in public, though as recently as 1942 the Court said unanimously that of course there was no constitutional problem with barring the lewd, the profane, or the obscene, because they weren't ideas.

*Therefore they weren't protected by the free-speech clause?*

That's right. The original meaning of the speech clause was the protection of ideas and the circulation of ideas, not the protection of self-gratification through pornography and other stuff. In fact, in the early cases, the pornographers, when they were prosecuted, didn't even raise the First Amendment, because nobody thought it was relevant. I think that's a big cultural shift the Court has worked on us.

*What would the response be from an ACLU lawyer?*

You are inhibiting my liberty and my right to express myself. And the answer to that is yes, that is precisely what we are after. We're talking almost entirely about obscenity in various forms. We're not talking about anything else.

*The fact is, we have a hard time censoring parts of rap music that are so obviously detrimental to African-American culture.*

It's detrimental to everybody's culture. Some of those rappers are white, and 75 percent of the best-selling rap records are sold to white suburban teenagers. Which tells you a couple of things, one of them being the collapse of moral courage. Where are their parents? Why haven't they said to them, "Get that stuff out of here and don't ever listen to it again"? They don't.

*Some have argued that moral and cultural decline or renewal are not really affected by the law or by politics. Do you agree?*

Politics is not the same as culture. Even if we had a conservative President and a conservative Congress, that would not affect what is taking place in the universities, in Hollywood, the network news, and so forth. Politics has an indirect bearing on culture, because a President, for example, can use the bully pulpit of the presidency to influence attitudes. Whether he can influence them more than the universities and television is a highly dubious proposition. . . .

## Resistance Is Needed

*Can this culture in decline turn itself around?*

I'm sure it can, but whether it will is a much harder question. The signs aren't good. I think if enough people who are aware of the kind of thing I describe in the book—that our culture is in decline in almost every area, from popular music to religion—and if they realized there was a common cause to this, they might begin to resist what is happening. When I say "resist," I don't mean trying to elect a President or anything as grand as that. They might try to resist it in their public schools, they might try to resist it in their church, they might try to resist it in the universities where they work. By and large, the people who are making this cultural attack are a minority, even in the universities. But they are activists, and they control the dialogue.

> "The original meaning of the speech clause was the protection of ideas, . . . not the protection of self-gratification through pornography."

The other thing is that there may be signs of a religious renewal in this country. It's not quite clear that there is, but Promise Keepers clearly reflects a religious impulse. The evangelical movement is certainly growing stronger. And one can hope that the more orthodox people in Catholicism, Protestantism, and Judaism will stiffen their spines and do battle in those denominations.

# Excluding Offensive Materials from Libraries Is Appropriate

**by S.M. Hutchens**

**About the author:** *S.M. Hutchens is a research associate for the* Religion & Society Report, *a monthly publication of the Howard Center for Family, Religion & Society in Rockford, Illinois.*

Winston Churchill said democracy is the best of all bad forms of government. In that spirit one might venture to say that most people who are ruled by the votes of popular majorities praise democracy, but try to get around it whenever possible. Everyone knows there is nothing that ails them that couldn't be fixed in pretty short order by a good stiff dose of privilege, as long as it is exercised by People Like Us. Given the givens, however, the best the anti-democratic democrat can do is cage for the power to flout the public will. Librarians are no exception and control as much ground as they can by screaming Censorship (which is always presumed immoral, and darkly made out to be unconstitutional whenever possible) when their privilege of determining what should be in the collection is questioned.

## Librarians vs. Parents

Probably the most dangerous and provocative enemy faced by the librarian, short of penny-pinching legislatures, is the mother who is not happy that her child, loose in the public library, has come home with a book illustrating the how-to's of oral sex. The library is typically unapologetic. *Caveat lector:* It has no right to censor what the public reads, and the child is a member of the public. Nor does the distraught mother have the moral right to insist it be removed from the collection. If she doesn't like it, other people do, so who is she to say it shouldn't be there? If she insists on making an issue of it, she is accused of censorship and made out to be not only a reactionary crank, but a crank who

Reprinted from S.M. Hutchens, "Marian the Totalitarian," *Religion & Society Report*, April 1998, with permission.

doesn't properly supervise her children in libraries.

On entering library school I came into my first serious contact with a profession valiant against "censorship." A question that began to bother me then, bothers me even more now that I am a librarian, and which I still ask with some frequency is why, when a librarian doesn't like a book and takes steps to see it doesn't appear in the collection, is this called "weeding" or "deselection," or "declining to purchase," while if someone else attempts the same thing it is called "censorship"? The truth of the assertion is so

> *"There is . . . no 'right to read'. . . in the sense of a right for librarians to choose whatever they think their collections should hold."*

evident I have never heard it denied by anyone confronted with it. When it is defended, it is almost always on the basis of the librarian's superior powers of discernment, that is, on her professional ability to decide what are and are not appropriate books—or perhaps now we should say, information sources—for the community she serves. Marian the Librarian, who knows that Rabelais and Balzac ought to be made available to the youth of River City over the objections of their parents, is alive and well, and is now beginning, with the well-financed support of groups like the American Library Association and the American Civil Liberties Union (ACLU) to dish them up the succulent delights of the Internet. ("Mommy, why's that lady wearing nothing but chains, and what's that man doing to her?")

## Librarians Serve the Community

What is obscured in all of this is the community's freedom in a democracy to determine what its library shall contain. The Mrs. Shinns of this world, as backward and belligerent as they may be, are within their rights to have the books removed if they can bring sufficient legal authority to bear on the matter. That people have the freedom under the Constitution to read or view pretty much what they want is not under dispute here. What is at issue is that public librarians should regard their selection of library materials as a professional privilege rather than a public trust, delegated to them by the representatives of the community they serve, and, subject to law, entirely responsible to the desires of that community. There is, in other words, no "right to read" or "right to view" in the sense of a right for librarians to choose whatever they think their collections should hold against the wishes of the people who have hired them to be the custodians of their information sources. To say otherwise is something like a cook claiming the professional privilege of telling his employer what he shall eat for dinner, whether he likes it or not. While the patron may tell the cook to go ahead and choose for him, something has gone wrong when the cook presumes to dictate what the plate will and will not hold.

Part of living in a democracy that galls a great many people, liberals and conservatives alike, is that ultimately things are under the control of the damned public, which is always stupider and more immoral than we are. My own opinions on what should be available in a public library, or the conditions under which they are to be made available, will almost always differ in some respect from those of the majority, in which case I must deal with the resultant library collection as best I can. Invariably there will be things there I do not like, or, even more seriously, things to which I do not wish browsing children, mine or anybody else's, to be exposed.

But let us be clear about three things: First, the attempt to circumvent the rights of the people by creating professional privilege that can stand against the public will is repugnant to a democracy. Librarians (and their professional associations) are no more to be trusted on this account than any other power lobby. Second, any reputed "right to read" does not stand for a public library's mandate to purchase materials that its public doesn't want in the collection. Third, opposing a library's materials selection in the name of public decency is no more shameful than insisting on ordinances insuring that people remain clothed on the streets.

## The Public's Right to Dictate Policy

There are two sides to the coin of the library's being a servant to "all the people." The one some librarians don't like is that the public has, within the confines of the law, the right to dictate policy, including collection policy, to the library. Bringing lawful pressure to bear upon the library board and administration to have offensive materials removed is just that—lawful—and may come to be regarded as a valuable service to the community if it turns out that community opinion differs from that of the library.

As for me, I don't want books made available to children in the general collection depicting oral sex any more than I want the same acts to be seen in other public places frequented by children, and would vote for any mayor who promises a library board that is not afraid to "censor" such materials. Having been among librarians for many years now, I am not the slightest bit impressed or intimidated by their cries of censorship, and join the many people in my profession—almost always shouted down by its radical representatives—who understand that the public library is a creature of its public before it is the property of the librarian, the American Library Association, or the ACLU.

> *"Bringing lawful pressure to bear upon the library board and administration to have offensive materials removed is just that—lawful."*

# Racist Speech Should Be Restricted

## by Richard Delgado

**About the author:** *Richard Delgado is the Charles Inglis Thomson Professor of Law at the University of Colorado School of Law. He is the coeditor of* The Price We Pay: The Case Against Racist Speech, Hate Propaganda, and Pornography *and the coauthor of* Must We Defend Nazis? Hate Speech, Pornography, and the New First Amendment.

At the University of Wisconsin, a fraternity sponsored an annual "Fiji Island" party, as part of which it erected a 15-foot plywood caricature of a black man with a bone through his nose. At Dartmouth College, four members of a conservative campus newspaper compared the university president, James O. Freedman, a Jew, with Adolf Hitler. At the University of California at Berkeley, fraternity members shouted obscenities and racial slurs at a group of black students; later, a campus disc jockey told black students who had requested that the station play rap music to "go back to Oakland." In Mississippi, a lesbian couple trying to establish a rural retreat was hounded by threatening messages and phone calls, and a dead chicken with an obscene note was attached to their mailbox.

These cases are not atypical. More than 300 American universities have experienced racial incidents serious enough to be reported by the media, and every year the FBI reports thousands of hate crimes and violence directed against Jews, gays and members of racial minorities. It is unlikely that the number of incidents is merely the result of increased sensitivity on the part of minority groups or better reporting, since it occurs at a time when other Western nations are reporting a wave of Holocaust revisionism and attacks on Jews and minorities.

## Speech Codes Are a Good Idea

More than 200 American universities have responded by enacting student-conduct codes penalizing face-to-face insults and epithets, while courts have developed sexual-harassment doctrine for women badgered and insulted in the workplace. Are these measures a good idea? Emphatically, yes: Racist and similar taunts convey little of value. They demean the victim while communicating to all who hear the message that equal personhood is of little value in American society. Campuses and workplaces wherein a climate of racial or sexual terror thrives are unattractive and unwelcoming for members of the victimized groups. Minority enrollment at many campuses drops in the months and years following well-publicized incidents of racial insult.

> *"Racist and similar taunts convey little of value."*

Rules against hate speech, homophobic remarks and misogyny serve both symbolic and institutional values—increasing productivity in the workplace and protecting a learning environment on campus. It has been argued that such prohibitions operate in derogation of the First Amendment's guarantee of freedom of speech, but that amendment already is subject to dozens of exceptions—libel, defamation, words of conspiracy or threat, disrespectful words uttered to a judge or police officer, irrelevant or untrue words spoken in a judicial proceeding, copyright, plagiarism, official secrets, misleading advertising and many more. The social interest in deterring vicious racial or sexual vituperation certainly seems at least as great as that underlying these other forms of speech deemed unworthy of First Amendment protection.

Some argue that speech codes are not as good a remedy to racist speech as talking back to the aggressor. According to this view, talking back will teach minorities not to rely on whites for protection while educating the utterer of a racially hurtful remark so that he or she will refrain from repeating the offense. But talking back can be futile or dangerous, especially when racist remarks are hurled, as they often are, in many-on-one situations or in cowardly fashion—a leaflet slipped under a black student's dormitory door. Talking back cannot be the sole remedy for a victim of racist hate speech.

## A Simplistic Argument

A third argument for tolerance of offensive utterances is that they serve as a kind of pressure valve, allowing tension to release itself before reaching a dangerous level. Forcing racists (homophobes, etc.) to bottle up their emotions means that they are more likely to do or say something even more harmful later. Anti-hate-speech rules, then, would increase, not reduce, minorities' jeopardy.

This argument is simplistic. Hate speech may well make the speaker feel better, but it does not make the victim safer. Social science teaches that permitting a person to do or say something hateful to another increases, not reduces, the chance that he or she will do so again. Moreover, others may feel that they can follow suit. Human behavior is more complex than the laws of physics that describe pressure valves, tanks and other mechanical things. Instead, society uses symbols to construct a social world, one that contains categories and expectations for terms such as "black," "woman," "gang member" and "child." Once these categories are in place, they govern perception and a sense of how folks may act toward others. Allowing persons to stigmatize and revile others makes them more aggressive toward those others in the future. Once a speaker comes to think of the other as a deserved victim, his or her behavior may escalate to bullying and physical violence.

Stereotypical behavior often generalizes: Action teaches others that they may act as well. Pressure valves may be safer after letting off steam; human beings are not. The experience of Canada, England, Germany, Sweden, Italy and other European countries that have enacted laws against racial revilement shows that incidents against minorities do not increase, but decrease, in the wake of passage.

## Speech and Social Reform

Other critics of speech codes argue that the First Amendment has been a great friend and ally of social reformers. The national president of the American Civil Liberties Union, for example, has argued that without free speech the Rev. Martin Luther King Jr. could not have moved America as he did—and so also for the environmental movement, women's rights and gay liberation. This argument is paternalistic: If minorities understood their best interest, the argument goes, they would not limit speech.

But the relationship of the First Amendment to social advance is not nearly so straightforward as some think. True, in the 1960s, King and others did use speech to kindle con-

*"Talking back cannot be the sole remedy for a victim of racist hate speech."*

science. As often as not, however, the First Amendment, as then understood and interpreted, did not protect them. They marched, were arrested and convicted; sat-in, were arrested and convicted; rallied and sang, were arrested and convicted. Their speech was deemed too forceful, too disruptive. To be sure, their convictions sometimes would be reversed years later on appeal, at the cost of thousands of dollars and hundreds of hours of gallant lawyering. Speech may have been a useful tool for racial reformers; the free-speech clause was not.

Would hate-speech laws inevitably lead to reverse enforcement? Would authorities overlook the more serious offenses of the sort mentioned in the first paragraph of this essay, while cracking down with a vengeance on the black motorist who utters something mildly disrespectful to the cop who stops him for a routine offense? This concern is plausible, because some authorities do overcharge blacks and other minorities with various offenses, including loitering. But the American experience with hate-speech rules shows that this has not been the usual pattern. Nor has it been elsewhere. A host of Western democracies have instituted laws against hate speech and crime. Some, such as Sweden, Great Britain and Canada, have traditions of respect for free speech and inquiry rivaling ours. In none has there been a noticeable erosion of the spirit of free inquiry nor a wave of prosecutions against blacks and immigrants.

If reverse enforcement occasionally happens, it is not necessarily a bad thing. If, in fact, a black or Mexican has terrorized or harassed a fellow student who is white, gay, or Asian, universities should bring charges: Minorities need to learn to speak respectfully, too. And if the fear is that college deans and administrators are so racist that they will invent or magnify charges against minority students in order to punish or hound them off campus, this is entirely implausible. Figures from *U.S. News & World Report* show that college administrators and faculty harbor less antiblack animus than the average American, even than the average college student. Indeed, it is the very concern of college administrators about dwindling minority enrollments and a worsening campus climate for minorities that underlies enactment of most hate-speech rules.

It also has been claimed that hate speech should not be driven underground but allowed to remain out in the open, since the racist one does not know is more dangerous than the one whom one does know. This argument ignores a third alternative—the racist who is cured, or at least deterred by official rules and the fear of sanction from exhibiting the behavior he or she once did. Since most conservatives (indeed most people) believe that laws and penalties change conduct, they ought to concede that institutional guidelines against hate speech and assault would discourage those behaviors.

## Playing the Victim?

A final objection is that prohibitions against verbal abuse and assault encourage minorities to see themselves as victims. Instead of running to campus authorities every time something wounds their feelings, persons of color ought to learn either to confront or ignore the offensive behavior. A system of hate-speech rules proclaims that minorities are weak and in need of protection, that their lot in life is to be victimized rather than to take charge of their own destinies. Will hate-speech rules have these effects? No, because other alternatives, such as talking back, will remain. No gay or minority student is required to file charges under the rules when targeted by abuse. The rules merely provide one more avenue of recourse for those who wish to take advantage of them. Filing a complaint might, indeed, be seen as one way of taking charge of one's destiny: One is active instead of passively "lumping it" when invective strikes. It is worth noticing that we do not raise the victimization issue with other offenses we suffer, such as having a car stolen or a house burglarized, or tell the victim to "rise above it." Could it be because we secretly believe that the black targeted in this fashion has not suffered a real harm? If so, this is quite different from saying that filing a complaint increases victimization. Besides, it is quite untrue: Racial invective harms; filing a civil complaint does not.

> *"It is the very concern . . . about . . . a worsening campus climate for minorities that underlies enactment of most hate-speech rules."*

None of the arguments against hate-speech rules, then, holds water. The rules are straightforward, wholly laudable ways of protecting values society holds dear. The right of the bigot to spew racial venom, like the right to punch someone in the nose, must yield in the face of other interests. Canada, Sweden, France, Italy and many other advanced societies have come to the same conclusion. Hate-speech rules are wholly consistent with the spirit of free inquiry. Indeed, by demoralizing the victim and excluding him or her from the human community, hate speech reduces participation and dialogue. Far from diminishing the values of the First Amendment, hate-speech rules may be necessary for their full flowering and effectuation.

> *"The right of the bigot to spew racial venom, like the right to punch someone in the nose, must yield in the face of other interests."*

# Violent and Pornographic Music Lyrics Should Be Restricted

by C. Delores Tucker

**About the author:** *C. Delores Tucker is the chair of the National Political Congress of Black Women, an organization that advocates on behalf of African-American women and their families.*

*Editor's note: This viewpoint was originally delivered before the Senate Subcommittee on Oversight of Government Management, Restructuring and the District of Columbia on November 6, 1997.*

I speak as Chair of the National Political Congress of Black Women, Inc., a nonprofit, nonpartisan organization for the political and economic empowerment of African-American women and their families.

I am pleased this arm of Congress is taking the time to address the urgent problem of "The Social Impact of Music Violence," a subject that I and the NPCBW have been engaged for more than five years in a relentless struggle to persuade the giant music industry to stop the production and worldwide distribution of violent, pornographic gangsta rap music. Those malicious lyrics grossly malign black women, degrade the unthinking young black artists who create it, pander pornography to our innocent young children, hold black people (especially young black males) universally up to ridicule and contempt, and corrupt its vast audience of listeners, white and black, throughout the world.

## Action Must Be Taken

I am filled with hope and anticipation because this Congressional body is holding a hearing. I trust and pray that you will follow through with positive action to save our children from the cultural scourges that are besieging them. I applaud the action Congress took to protect children from the cultural filth on

Reprinted from C. Delores Tucker's testimony before the U.S. Senate Committee on Governmental Affairs, Subcommittee on Oversight of Government Management, Restructuring, and the District of Columbia, November 6, 1997.

the Internet. The same concern and action is needed by Congress to protect the children from the violent and pornographic messages that are promoted to them over the airways and peddled to them in record stores. We say that action must be taken to curb and control the proliferation of this vile, demeaning and misogynistic music. We are not talking about censorship. Instead, we are talking about establishing guidelines for more responsive and responsible corporate citizenship. A corporation must be granted authority by a governmental body in order to exist. No

> *"The music industry started spending millions to promote and distribute music that teaches kids that it's cool to kill, use drugs, gang rape girls, and denigrate women."*

corporation should be allowed to exist if engaged in activities that contaminate and infect the minds of children. There are already laws in existence that protect children from pornography and exploitation. I beg of this body to clarify and strengthen the existing laws on the books so there is no doubt as to their intent and purpose.

We simply want some means or measure to stop the classic "yelling fire in a crowded theater"! We want to bring a return of civilized discourse in our musical art.

## Demeaning Filth

To black women, the depressing existence of drugs, violence and death in the black inner cities of this country is alarming. We are the grandmothers, mothers, sisters, aunts, cousins, sweethearts, wives, and family friends of the targeted black male—fathers gone, along with hope and jobs, streets filled with drugs, violence, death—those escaping this are headed for a new address—prisons—prisons, jails that are bulging with young black men, and now an increasing number of young black women. A recent report declared that one out of every four young black men is either in prison, on probation, or parole. I have deemed this the 3-P plague.

During the past five years, since the corporate moguls of the music industry started spending millions to promote and distribute music that teaches kids that it's cool to kill, use drugs, gang rape girls and denigrate women in the most vulgar and violent ways, jails are bulging and teenage drug use has increased four-fold.

Again, we say that we are not trying to tell the record industry how to conduct their business. We only want them to transform it—to stop it from the production of filth that demeans us as a race, corrupts our children and spreads this noxious poison. All America should take note—the poison exists not just in the inner cities, but is spreading to the more affluent suburbs as well.

We want the industry to respect us like they do others. For example, when pop star Michael Jackson included some words in his album, "They Don't Care

About Us" that our Jewish friends considered anti-Semitic, they protested, and Jackson was immediately forced to remove the offensive words. The Jewish complaints forced MTV to eliminate the song from its playlists! We want the industry to treat our complaints with the same promptness and respected concern! I applauded the Jewish leaders for their swift action. Black leaders should have made the same demands when this music first surfaced. . . .

## Preying on Black Artists

As I have said time and time again, the drug trade in the black community is fueling much that is ravaging our young people in abandoned communities. . . . There is no safety net there. Gangsta music is drugs-driven, race-driven, sex-driven, greed-driven and violence-driven. The wealthy mavens of the record industry—for example, Ted Field, heir to the Marshall Field fortune and owner of Interscope Records, Edgar Bronfman Jr., millionaire owner of Seagrams, who recently bought an interest in Interscope Records from Field—prey on the hapless and desperately poor, young black artists to produce gangsta rap filth and will simply accept nothing else. These young artists, many of them highly talented, living as they do in communities where there are no jobs, families are ripped apart, surviving where everything is bottomed out, are easy prey. Self-hate is all consuming. The desperate need for money and the life status it brings, reigns.

> *"Principle must come before profit."*

An example of how racism is undergirding gangsta Rap can be seen in the experiences of rapper Lichelle "Boss" Laws. As the *Wall Street Journal* article of February 3, 1994 reported, when Lichelle's style of rap was considered soft, she was told that she would not be produced unless her rap became hardcore with profanity. This has been true for many African-American artists seeking record contracts. Placing profit ahead of social obligation must cease.

I am saying that principle must come before profit. Congress has an obligation to the children and families of this nation to confront the music industry elite about the deplorable music products that they routinely indict upon society.

Permit me for a moment to share some quotes from Mrs. Coretta Scott King, Dr. Benjamin Hooks, former Executive Director of the National Association for the Advancement of Colored People (N.A.A.C.P.), and Rabbi Eric H. Yoffie.

Mrs. King stated, "Young people often look to performing artists for moral guidance and inspiration as well as entertainment but when these artists glorify guns and beatings they are injecting poison into the veins of America's future."

Dr. Hooks noted, "Our cultural experience does not include debasing our women, the glorification of violence, the promotion of deviant sexual behavior. This type of music is widely aberrant from the great music and musicians born of our culture and which have graced America."

Rabbi Yoffie stated in an open letter to the music industry that "The music is also profoundly racist, using black artists and targeting African-Americans as its major audience (although half of the records and CDs are sold to white kids in the suburbs). It presents blacks in stereotypical images: black people kill, commit violent acts, disdain family values, black men are predators. Black women are a special target, constantly referred to as 'bitches' and 'hos' (whores)."

## Stopping a Cultural Cancer

In closing, I wish to remind this body that banning the sale of violent misogynistic and pornographic music to our children is one preventive action Congress can take to curb violence. But it is one that is imperative to begin the process of healing our nation. NO ONE and NO INDUSTRY should be allowed to continue the social and psychological poisoning of the young minds of this nation that occurs with the music industry.

Finally, I say to you this day that there is a cultural cancer spreading through America. The sooner we recognize this, the sooner we can stop it before it becomes terminal. My organization and I have vowed to continue this fight to a successful conclusion. We hope that Congress will assist us in any way it can.

# The Media Must Exercise Self-Restraint

by Michael Eisner

**About the author:** *Michael Eisner is the chairman and CEO of the Walt Disney Company.*

"Congress shall make no law respecting an establishment of religion, or prohibiting the free exercise thereof; or abridging the freedom of speech, or of the press; or the right of the people peaceably to assemble, and to petition the Government for a redress of grievances." Employing just 45 words, the founding fathers managed to establish the freedom to pray any way you want—or not pray; say anything you want—well, almost anything; publish any ideas you want—of course libel is out; get together in any place you want—sort of; and if that's not enough, to complain to the government about anything else you want to complain about.

But no matter how many times the First Amendment is quoted, there is one key aspect of it that is consistently overlooked, an aspect that is of special significance to all of us who work in news and in entertainment: the First Amendment does not apply to us.

## Regulating the Government

Of course, I am well aware that we are all direct beneficiaries of the First Amendment. But our role is passive. The fact is that the amendment is not directed at us. It all goes back to the first of those 45 words, "Congress shall make no law. . . ." In other words, it is setting rules of behavior for the government, not for us. This makes the amendment all the more remarkable. After all, most legal documents dictate the behavior of citizens, instructing us on everything from how to drive our cars, to how to build our homes, to how to pay our taxes, to even how to protect corporate trademarks with large round ears.

The First Amendment does just the opposite. It regulates the government, and lets us be. This puts the United States in stark contrast to most other nations. Consider the words of Nelba Blandon, who was Nicaragua's Director of the Of-

Reprinted from Michael Eisner, "The Flip-Side of the First Amendment," *The Responsive Community*, Summer 1998, by permission of the author.

fice of Mass Media a decade ago. Here is what she had to say about the editorial content of one of Nicaragua's newspapers, *La Prensa:* "They accused us of suppressing freedom of expression. This was a lie and we could not let them publish it."

This is why I say the First Amendment does not apply to us. It applies to the would-be Nelba Blandons and keeps them off our backs, leaving us free to express ourselves as best we can.

## Hiding Behind the Constitution

Consider my own experience. I've been involved in the making of TV shows, movies, theme parks, and news. I've been involved in producing mediocre entertainment, good entertainment, occasionally great entertainment, and sometimes even important entertainment. At Paramount, we made "Reds," which was about the communist John Reed. At Disney, we made "Blaze," which was about Louisiana Governor Earl Long, and "Nixon". . . about Nixon. Never once did I think, "What will the president think?" or "What will a governor think?" or "What will a mayor or city council think?" I say this not because I am fearless, but because the First Amendment gives us nothing to fear.

What I do think about is how we in the media sometimes conveniently embrace the First Amendment. How many times have you seen entertainment executives justify the release of vile programs and repugnant lyrics by sanctimoniously proclaiming, "Freedom of speech"? This same self-serving behavior can be seen in the newspaper business as well, as certain publishers will print egregious material and then eagerly hide behind the skirts of the Constitution, saying, in effect, "The First Amendment made me do it."

> *"Since the government will not tell us what we can't do, we have to tell* ourselves *what we can't do."*

I am sure that when we were all in school, we read the Bill of Rights often and thoroughly, and knew well that the first five words are, "Congress shall make no law," and realized that the First Amendment limits the government from acting repressively. We also learned, however, that the First Amendment does not give license to the media to act irresponsibly. Because the First Amendment does regulate the government, it has made our jobs much easier. But, at the same time, it has also made our jobs more challenging. The government has to allow freedom of expression; we have to make choices. We all have to be editors—journalists and entertainers alike. Since the government will not tell us what we can't do, we have to tell *ourselves* what we can't do.

## Tough Choices

This makes for tough choices. For example, in 1997 we recalled an album because we found the lyrics offensive. Because we are far from perfect, the album did get recorded and it did get released. When one of our executives brought the offensive lyrics to our attention, we took what we felt was the appropriate action.

Then there is a certain television show you may have heard of that in 1997 we decided to keep on the air, despite the fact that its star walked publicly out of the closet. It would have been very easy, instead, for The Walt Disney Company to simply walk away from the show. But, we didn't for a very simple reason: "Ellen" was a good show. It was creative, intelligent, well written and—of particular importance for a situation comedy—it was actually funny. Just recently it won the most coveted award in broadcasting—the

> *"There is a boundary . . . where fantasy, adventure, and escape turn to irresponsible depiction and inappropriate behavior."*

Peabody Award. In other words, our most controversial show passed the same test as arguably our least controversial show—"Home Improvement." It was creatively worthy, and we stuck by it.

There is a constant tension between allowing artists who work for us to have the right to free expression, and exercising personal responsibility regarding the content of the product we put out. These decisions are tough. But they are decisions that must be honestly confronted. We are dealing with the human core here. We know what is embarrassing, what makes us so anxious as to be unpleasant, what forces us to lose our poise and cover our face. Edit we must—not to stifle conflict or conviction, but to eliminate debasement.

I guess what I am talking about is good taste and good judgment. We are brought up to have it, then generally lose it during our teenage years, and hopefully get it back. The underlying issue is not content, but the way content is presented. Almost any subject can be dealt with tastefully in entertainment or in news; and almost any subject can be dealt with in ways that demean. Done well, all sorts of issues are worthy of exploration, from heterosexuality to homosexuality, from peace to violence, from infidelity to blissful marriage, from democracy to merciless oppression, from racial harmony to riots.

But there is a boundary—and, generally, we can all recognize where that line is—where fantasy, adventure, and escape turn to irresponsible depiction and inappropriate behavior. Short-term profits—even long-term profits—do not excuse clearly unethical decisions. Citizens fighting like hockey players on television over sexual infidelities; disc jockeys who make racial and incendiary comments; rock groups advocating violence on women and police—these all are permissible under the First Amendment, but they are not desirable if we aspire to call ourselves civilized.

## Avoiding the Race to the Bottom

Of course, the pressures are great to just join in. In all our businesses, a race to the bottom seems to be gaining momentum. But I believe that most of us are willing and wanting to head in a different direction. This is because we find that it is the high road that tends to take us to the best destinations, while the low road often leads to a dead end. Of course we all take detours, travel the dark at times rather than the light. But in the end, the light hopefully will prevail.

We are part of the civilized world, or at least we are supposed to be. Does not civilization depend on less brutality and aggression? We separate ourselves from the rest of the animal world by learning manners and poise and suppressing our primal instincts. And if all we do in creating intellectual product is feed those suppressed desires, we will simply be encouraging barbarity.

There is no exact formula to tell you what is right, and on occasion in the creative process content is produced that later you wish had never made it out of the editing room. But more often than not, diligent and thoughtful discussion results in quality programs. The fact is that quality generally does win out. From "Schindler's List" to "60 Minutes" to "Seinfeld" to "Beauty and the Beast," it is work of quality and honor that is valued in the long term.

> *"Does not civilization depend on less brutality and aggression?"*

The choice of the high road or the low road is one we all get to regularly make—thanks to the First Amendment. By not dictating the road we must take, it leaves us no choice but to choose for ourselves. It allows us to revel in responsibility, to strive to edit our careers—and our lives—wisely and well.

In the end, when we find ourselves on our deathbeds, I don't think we will say to our adoring family hovering nearby, "Do you remember that really salacious nude roller skater I put on the air back in '98? Wasn't that great television?" And I don't think our adoring spouses will smile and say, "Yes dear, that was wonderful." If we keep this in mind, I think we'll all do all right.

# Free Speech Should Not Be Limited

**by Armstrong Williams**

**About the author:** *Armstrong Williams is a nationally syndicated columnist.*

*Editor's note: The following essay was originally published on Independence Day, July 4, 1997.*

As we celebrate 221 years of independence, I want to take this opportunity to challenge myself and others who have argued for curtailing free speech when it provokes hatred and fear: We need to reconsider the value in limiting one of the greatest freedoms we have been granted.

Our Constitution is the oldest written document of its kind. Freedom of speech, guaranteed by the First Amendment, has often been threatened but has withstood assault by those who would seek to deny us that right. It has proved to be one of our most important freedoms, but we must maintain constant vigilance so that neither it nor any other right is abused.

Interpretation of the First Amendment and what types of speech it protects have been argued for generations. Perhaps no other section of that great document has excited as much debate.

## Free Speech Is Essential to Democracy

Nowadays, we enjoy extraordinary freedom of expression and the right to say almost anything. This has not always been the case. It was not until recently that the protections granted by the First Amendment were broadly interpreted. In 1917, Judge Learned Hand first pointed out the necessity of free speech to a democratic society. At the time, cases involving the free speech component of the First Amendment dealt strictly with political statements.

Commenting on a case involving criticism of the war, he stated that the suppression of such statements, "and of all opinion except what encouraged and supported the existing policies . . . would contradict the normal assumption of democratic government."

What Hand was saying is that free speech is essential to a democratic system. In this, he mirrored James Madison's belief that the people possess absolute sovereignty.

The Constitution states that "Congress shall make no law . . ." but says nothing about what states may do. In the *New York Times vs. Sullivan*, the Supreme Court ruled in 1964 that states could not bar free speech any more than the federal government could. The Constitution guarantees the rights of all citizens. It is the law of the land, superseding state and local statutes.

## The Risk of Hypocrisy

Yet sometimes we wish people weren't so free to say whatever they want, however they want. When they express opinions with which we disagree, we wish they would keep quiet. When the subject is offensive, we wouldn't mind if they were penalized. But often we run the risk of hypocrisy. It is wrong to grant freedom of speech but then to qualify it by prohibiting dissenting opinions. This is an important point, and one we must remember on this national holiday.

How can we ever have new ideas if people are not free to speak their minds? We should never assume people are wrong before they open their mouths. How will I know where I am wrong, if you deny me the right to speak? Without dialogue, we can never hope to have understanding, and without understanding, we can never progress as a free people.

Congress passed the Alien and Sedition Acts in 1798, making it a crime to "write, print, utter or publish" anything negative about the government with intent to "defame or incite contempt or hatred of Congress or the president." At the time, it was deemed necessary to silence opposition against an expected war with France. The enactments proved a disaster, however, and Thomas Jefferson revoked the laws when he took office in 1801.

Can you imagine if such a law existed today? Our country would be in chaos. I think it is safe to say our fledgling nation would not have survived. Certainly, had those acts been allowed to stand, our world would be far different today.

Threats to our freedoms did not end there, however. Our entire history has been a struggle to guarantee inalienable rights to all Americans. America is the land of the free, but that freedom has not come easily. Many are still denied the same freedoms most of us take for granted. Without the guarantee of our Constitution, we

> **"It is wrong to grant freedom of speech but then to qualify it by prohibiting dissenting opinions."**

would be a sorry lot, afraid to do or say anything that might remotely cause harm to any group or individual. We certainly would not be the world's only superpower if that were the case.

So as we celebrate our independence this year, let us look back on where we have been and how far we have come. Let us not forget what it took to get us here. When we hear someone give an opinion we do not like or that is mean-spirited in some way, let us not jump up and muzzle the speaker, but thank God and the Constitution that we have freedom of expression and can believe what we wish.

As Thomas Jefferson said in his Inaugural address on March 4, 1801, let all those with whom we disagree "stand undisturbed as monuments of the safety with which error of opinion may be tolerated where reason is left free to combat it."

Reason, not laws, will show them the error of their ways.

# Children's Access to Library Materials Should Not Be Restricted

by Robert Riehemann

**About the author:** *Robert Riehemann is an adjunct faculty member in the mathematics department at Thomas More College in Fort Mitchell, Kentucky.*

Recall your childhood. Imagine trying to check out a book from your local library on the big bang or evolution. Suppose that you were told that a parent would have to check it out for you because it was from the adult section. (Say it was *The Eyewitness Visual Dictionary of the Universe* by Dorling Kindersley Limited or *Fossils Tell of Long Ago* by Aliki.) It might even be necessary to read from these books to complete a science homework assignment. Would your rights as a child and library patron have been violated? Not according to the Attorney General of the State of Alabama, Jimmy Evans. The forms that are used to permit such restrictions in the White Smith Library of Alabama are before me. They were sent to me after I attended the inaugural meeting for Family Friendly Libraries (FFL) in October 1995.

## Excessive Restrictions

Ostensibly, this group is motivated by concerns over the sexual content of material available to minors. In particular, President Karen Jo Gounaud has described material that is favorable to homosexuals as philosophically radical and not family friendly. Since I know that my extended family includes practicing homosexuals, I would like to see my children understand something of this lifestyle to permit them to include and welcome these members into their family. So I don't really see Gounaud's point. Yet the FFL inaugural meeting included a speaker whose only topic was the infiltration of homosexuals into the card catalogue. Indeed, now there are ways to obtain information about homosexuals without passing through the evaluative comments of "sexual perver-

Reprinted from Robert Riehemann, "Family Friendly Libraries," *Free Inquiry*, Spring 1997, by permission of *Free Inquiry*. Endnotes in the original have been omitted in this reprint.

sion" or "sexual deviation." What a broadside to morality, the very fabric of the republic is thus torn!

This speaker even suggested during lunch that such problems arose because homosexuals have occupied high places in the library power structure. I was left with the impression that homosexuals should be barred from such positions. (And while we are making homosexuals second-class citizens, perhaps we could do some-thing about the Jews, atheists, and mentally impaired. I believe there is some historical precedent in Germany.)

> *"There are limits to the restriction of the rights of others, even if those others are your children."*

It is certainly valid for any group of people to organize and approach their locally controlled library with issues of concern. Yet there are limits to the restriction of the rights of others, even if those others are your children. The belief that it should be possible to prevent a child from reading science, medical information, or competing religious views is patently absurd. If a parent wishes to thus restrict a child, handcuffing him or her to a bedpost will do as nicely. Yet, during the meeting, it was pointed out that the kind of restrictions envisioned by FFL could prevent a child's access to books by or about Bertrand Russell, Thomas Aquinas, Martin Luther, and Muhammad or information about the big bang or evolution. This could be motivated by the parent's religious views only. Gounaud remarked that such things are best left to the discretion of parents. She emphasized after the meeting that "anything goes" regarding restrictions by parents. Is this true?

As an intellectual giant among the Founding Fathers, Thomas Jefferson dealt with issues in almost every field. Censorship was one of them. In the early part of the nineteenth century, he bought a volume by de Becourt entitled *"Sur la Creation du Monde, un Systeme d'Organisation Primitive."* Interestingly, this volume instigated a criminal inquiry as an offense against religion. In a letter to his bookseller, N. G. Dufief, Jefferson expressed his mortification that such a thing could happen in the United States of America. He went on to say:

> Is this then our freedom of religion? And are we to have a censor whose imprimatur shall say what books may be sold, and what we may buy? And who is thus to dogmatize religious opinions for our citizens? Whose foot is to be the measure to which ours are all to be cut or stretched? Is a priest to be our inquisitor, or shall a layman, simple as ourselves, set up his reason as the rule for what we are to read, and what we must believe? It is an insult to our citizens to question whether they are rational beings or not, and blasphemy against religion to suppose it cannot stand the test of truth and reason. If M. de Becourt's book be false in its facts, disprove them; if false in its reasoning, refute it. But, for God's sake, let us freely hear both sides, if we choose. . . ."

I wonder if such sentiments should apply to children in libraries. The alternative seems to be the public funding of religiously motivated censorship, a fearful prospect.

## The Danger of Restricted Reading

Recall that the assassination of Yitzak Rabin was religiously motivated and evidently supported by rabbinical interpretations of the Jewish religious laws known as *halacha*. It is not unreasonable, in my view, to believe that restricted reading and participation in a closed and segregated social group can contribute greatly to such a disaster. And this is exactly what the FFL permits: the policing of reading matter by parents through the agency of the library. It should be stopped.

An article on the Rabin assassination in the *New York Review of Books* by Amos Elon lends support to this idea. It details the extremist circles that the self-confessed assassin traveled and also the narrow interpretation of *halacha* that "justified" the murder. Elon then quotes a member of the National Religious Party of Israel who publicly observed that, "It is an undeniable fact that nearly all violent right-wing extremists in Israel today are wearing skullcaps and are graduates of religious educational institutions. We must ask ourselves where we have gone wrong." Let's not permit the further segregation of religious fundamentalists in the United States through the agency

> *"It is an insult to our citizens to question whether they are rational beings or not."*

of the FFL. We are one nation and to stay that way, we need a free and open society with free libraries.

In late 1996, Karen Jo Gounaud spoke to the southeastern section of the American Library Association in Lexington, Kentucky. On request, she sent about 175 pages of material about FFL and the issues involved. Most of this is naturally derived from the religious right since it was from such groups that she obtained the seed money to create her organization. She included a two-page list of creation science resources and about twelve pages of advertisements for children's books promoting Christian lifestyles. Her literature makes me doubt very much that she would recommend that these books be placed on a restricted access list. Rather she would argue that they represent local community values. In this way, Gounaud would do the thinking for my children. Frankly, I would rather see them think for themselves.

# Racist Speech Should Not Be Restricted

## by Jacob Sullum

**About the author:** *Jacob Sullum is a syndicated columnist and a senior editor for* Reason, *a monthly libertarian magazine.*

In the Norman Rockwell painting "Freedom of Speech," an earnest Everyman stands at a public meeting to offer a question or comment. Judging from his mild expression and the polite attention of the people around him, he is not saying anything offensive or threatening.

Maybe he is asking for a new stop sign, complaining about an unfilled pothole or suggesting a raffle to raise money for the next Founders' Day celebration. Whatever it is, chances are he'd be able to say it without a constitutional guarantee.

The painting nicely captures how most Americans view the First Amendment, which they love in theory but often abhor in practice. They are proud to protect freedom of speech, as long as the speech does not stray too far from Rockwell's warm and fuzzy image.

### An Inflammatory Pamphlet

The pamphlet that got nine Florida high school students arrested in late February 1998 was anything but warm and fuzzy. The 20-page, mostly handwritten booklet ridiculed people with "African diseases" and a weak grasp of English. It included drawings depicting a rape, a head with a bloody fork sticking out of it, and the school's black principal, Timothy Dawson, impaled on a dart board. "What would happen if I shot Dawson in the head?" mused the author of an article entitled "A Student's Complaint."

Five girls and four boys distributed about 2,500 copies of the pamphlet at Killian High School in Kendall, a Miami suburb. For disrupting school with this inflammatory material, they were suspended, which is pretty much what you'd expect. But they were also arrested and charged with a felony, which transformed a local embarrassment into a national news story.

Reprinted from Jacob Sullum, "First Amendment Also Protects Rubbish," *Conservative Chronicle*, March 18, 1998, by permission of Jacob Sullum and Creators Syndicate.

The teenagers ran afoul of a 1945 criminal libel law prohibiting anonymous publication of material that "tends to expose any individual or any religious group to hatred, contempt, ridicule or obloquy." Florida's "hate crime" law, which enhances penalties for offenses motivated by animosity toward a racial, ethnic or religious group, bumped this first-degree misdemeanor up to a third-degree felony. The Killian High pamphleteers therefore faced a penalty of up to five years in prison.

## The Right to Incite Racism

Since he was personally attacked in the pamphlet, the principal's overreaction is perhaps understandable. It's harder to fathom why the school district defended his decision to throw the kids in jail. "The arrests were made, and we stand by that decision," said Henry Fraind, deputy superintendent for Miami-Dade County Public Schools. "They do not have the right to incite the feelings of outward racism."

The thing is, they do. The First Amendment protects both the right to engage in anonymous speech and the right to express racist views. There's no question that Florida's criminal libel law would be overturned by the courts if it were challenged.

The state attorney in Miami acknowledged as much a few days after the arrests, when she said her office had dropped the charges because Supreme Court rulings "render the

> *"The First Amendment protects . . . the right to express racist views."*

statute in question unconstitutional and unenforceable." She nevertheless defended the arrests saying, "This has been a difficult decision because the document in question does contain language and drawings of an outrageous and highly offensive nature."

The decision should not have been difficult. It's scary that the chief prosecutor in a major American city seems to think that the question of whether people can be jailed for something they said hinges on how outrageous it was. After all, when speech is punished, it's usually because it offended someone.

## Garbage Must Be Tolerated

Seduced by a Norman Rockwell vision of the First Amendment, Americans too often forget that freedom of expression was a controversial notion for most of human history not because our ancestors were benighted fools but because they recognized that speech is often pernicious. The classical liberals who opposed censorship did not claim that all speech was equally worthwhile, but they did insist that a central authority could not be trusted to sort the good from the bad.

That conviction means we are obliged to tolerate all sorts of garbage, some of it much worse than the puerile rag distributed at Killian High School. Sadly, the students who produced the pamphlet, which included an excerpt from the First Amendment, seemed to understand that point better than school administrators or local law enforcement officials.

The authorities may have hoped that a night in jail would teach these kids a lesson, but instead it transformed a bunch of obnoxious jerks into free-speech martyrs. Call them the Killian 9.

# Music Lyrics Should Not Be Censored

## by Jim D'Entremont

**About the author:** *Jim D'Entremont is the head of the Boston Coalition for Freedom of Expression.*

In February 1997, the goth-rock ensemble Marilyn Manson and its eponymous lead singer embarked on a circuit of North American concert venues to promote the album *Anti-Christ Superstar*. As embroidered accounts of the band's performances passed into fact, the disapproval of the pious quickly spiralled into panic. The band's musical stagings were said to incorporate devil worship, live sex, defilement of Bibles, flag desecration, animal slaughter and Grand Guignol effects of indescribably blasphemous obscenity. Circulars produced in Tupelo, Mississippi by the Reverend Donald Wildmon's American Family Association (AFA) warned that Marilyn Manson 'wants to put an end to Christianity through his music.'

## Zealots Protest

Marilyn Manson's pungent fusion of gender-bending and the occult provided a powerful organising and fundraising tool for ideologues whose power base is ignorance infused with fear. Protest demonstrations were assembled in cities throughout the USA by zealots across the sectarian spectrum. Cancellation of a Utah booking triggered a lawsuit. The fundamentalists of Oklahomans for Children and Families tried forcefully but vainly to stop the band from appearing in Oklahoma City. In Indiana, a movement arose to 'bind' the demons of Marilyn Manson through prayer.

When the group joined OzzFest, a concert package headlined by Ozzy Osbourne, the much-reviled former lead singer of Black Sabbath, protests escalated. 'Hate-Rock Rolls Across Country', screamed the *AFA Journal*. In New Jersey, OzzFest had to obtain a legal injunction to honour a performance date; in Virginia, the show was cancelled. Adopting a tactic increasingly popular among Christian activists, the Minnesota Family Council targeted the

Reprinted, with permission, from Jim D'Entremont, "The Devil's Disciples," originally published in the June 1998 issue of *Index on Censorship*. For more information contact: Tel.: 44 (171) 278-2313; Fax: 44 (171) 278-1878; Email: contact@indexoncensorship.org; or visit www.oneworld.org/index_oc.

Minneapolis-based Best Buy Company, sponsor of OzzFest, for a boycott. The AFA urged its 350,000 members to distribute information endorsing the boycott and to ask their friends to take 'Christian action'.

Political analyst Richard Hofstadter notes that in the USA the extreme right has demonstrated 'how much political leverage can be got out of the passions of a small minority'. A network of right-wing authoritarian movements whose alliances are often weak, the theocratic right has far less popular support than it claims to command. Yet it remains one of the most potent antidemocratic forces ever to emerge in the USA. Its adherents are committed to erasing the separation of church and state that is the cornerstone of US democracy. Most of these faith-propelled reactionaries are Protestants—evangelicals, hard-shell Baptists, Pentecostals, members of charismatic sects—united by belief in the unerring literal truth of the Bible, in apocalyptic prophecy, and in justice as clean, swift, merciless and mighty as Jehovah's thunderbolt.

The theocratic right brings true believers into frequently unwitting partnerships with those who know that fear of God's wrath and Satan's guile can be brokered into power and financial gain. Nina Crowley, president of the Massachusetts Music Industry Coalition (Mass MIC), observes that 'while many religious groups may have been founded on lofty moral guidelines, long ago their interest in enlightening society mutated into that of controlling society both morally and politically.' In its pursuit of such ends, the movement is at odds with tenets of free speech articulated in the First Amendment to the US Constitution.

## Abstract Principles vs. Cultural Biases

The American political tradition that sanctifies abstract principles of free expression is often at war with its cultural biases in favour of repression. Those biases took root in seventeenth-century Puritan New England and set the tone for the cultural life of colonial America. To most of the American Founding Fathers, art in any form was suspect. A tradition of philistine censoriousness, both religious and secular, has been a constant in US culture.

Beginning in the post–Civil War era, moral crusades led by Anthony Comstock continued into the twentieth century. As soon as jazz began to surface, it was demonised. In August 1921, Anne Shaw Faulkner of the General Federation of Women's Clubs, a bulwark of American Protestantism, published 'Does Jazz Put the Sin in Syncopation?' in the *Ladies Home Journal*. Shaw characterized jazz as 'the accompaniment of the voodoo dancer, stimulating the half-crazed barbarian to the vilest deeds.' By the 1930s, when this uniquely American music had achieved international recognition as an art form, many Americans nonetheless agreed with the Nazi assessment of jazz as *entartete*—decadent—music.

> *"To most of the American Founding Fathers, art in any form was suspect."*

*Chapter 2*

## Fear of Rock

The racism inherent in Faulkner's appraisal of jazz pervaded white attitudes toward rhythm and blues. As a white derivative of black R&B, rock and roll was denounced from the time of its birth in the early 1950s. Southern segregationists like Asa Carter of the North Alabama White Citizens Council complained that rock arose from a Jewish-Marxist plot to drag white youth 'down to the level of the Negro'.

Fear of rock was not confined to Southern bigots. By 1955, 'jungle music' was at the apex of a moral panic over 'juvenile delinquency'. US Senate hearings publicised the virulence of youth-oriented mass media. Clerics of all denominations expressed concern that music was turning American teens into savages. In 1958, the Catholic Youth Center implored its members to destroy whatever records in their possession promoted 'a pagan concept of life'. According to Billy James Hargis's Christian Crusade, rock music was part of a 'systematic plan geared to making a generation of American youth mentally ill and emotionally unstable.'

No amount of alarmist moral rearmament could curb the popularity of Elvis Presley, whose greatest fans belonged to the same Southern white Protestant culture that spawned his most ardent detractors, or of the Beatles, who rode a wave of Anglophilia into worldwide adulation. In 1966,

> *"No amount of alarmist moral rearmament could curb the popularity of Elvis Presley."*

however, when John Lennon imprudently told the *London Evening Standard* that Christianity 'will vanish' and that the Beatles were 'more popular than Jesus now', these statements offended US fundamentalists more vitally than the Beatles' freewheeling attitudes toward sex and drugs. A wave of record-burnings ensued, continuing even after Lennon, fated to be assassinated 14 years later by a born-again Christian, issued an apology.

## "The Work of Satan"

By 1969, as music began to reflect the general relaxation in censorship, religious anti-rock crusaders could point to a wealth of drug allusions and an increase of profanity. Billy James Hargis's associate David A Noebel, who now heads Summit Ministries in Colorado, was a key proponent of paranoid Christian thinking with regard to music. Author of such diatribes as *Communism, Hypnotism, and the Beatles* (1965), Noebel feared that rock would make 'a generation of American youth useless through nerve-jamming, mental deterioration and retardation.' Prefiguring theorists of backward-masking and subliminal indoctrination, he insisted that capitalism was being undermined by hidden messages in rock songs. Noebel's findings were supported by Bob Larson's *Rock and Roll: The Devil's Diversion* (1967), which identified the beat of rock as the direct work of Satan. This was the first of a succession of books in which

Larson, still active as a lecturer and radio personality, would warn against 'rock's symbiosis with Satanism'.

In the late 1970s, Florida minister Charles Boykin began systematically burning thousands of records, and Steve and Dan Peters of St Paul, Minnesota, formed Truth About Rock, an organisation whose inaugural event was a bonfire of musical vanities. The Peters brothers still deliver addresses to schools, youth groups, and evangelical gatherings in which they encourage record-burning. In this period, televangelism was beginning to awaken the political consciousness of Pentecostals and Baptists. Fans of Jerry Falwell's *Old Time Gospel Hour* provided a membership base for the short-lived but iconic Moral Majority; the constituency of Pat Robertson's *700 Club* later became the core of the more durable Christian Coalition. Popular music continues to be a convenient scapegoat for the followers of both Falwell and Robertson.

> *"Christian commentators stress that cult leader Charles Manson was an aspiring musician; serial killer Richard Ramirez was an AC/DC fan."*

In 1984, Rick Alley, a Cincinnati businessman incensed by Prince's sexually explicit lyrics, proposed a system of music ratings to help stamp out 'porn rock'. The Recording Industry Association of America (RIAA) ignored this campaign until it was adopted by Tipper Gore, wife of US Vice-President Albert Gore, then a senator from Tennessee. In response to purported obscenities in Prince's *Purple Rain* album, Mrs Gore assembled a coterie of her peers including Christian activist Susan Baker, wife of one of Ronald Reagan's cabinet officials and a national board member of James Dobson's Focus on the Family. Together they formed the Parents Music Resource Center (PMRC) in May 1985. Senate Commerce Committee hearings were convened four months later. Fearing government intervention, the RIAA endorsed a problematic, voluntary, industry-wide system of album-cover advisory labels warning parents of 'explicit lyrics'.

## Authoritarian Solutions

After the fall of communism, right-wing theocrats claimed that Satan was now focused on secular humanist efforts to undermine the US family through abortion, homosexuality, twisted art and sinister music. 'Contemporary music idolises death,' lament Tim and Beverly LaHaye in their book *A Nation Without a Conscience*. In *Learn to Discern,* Bob DeMoss, youth culture specialist for Focus on the Family, warns of bands who emphasise 'the morbid side of life'. These include AC/DC, Led Zeppelin, Judas Priest, KISS, Motley Crue and Slayer. Christian commentators stress that cult leader Charles Manson was an aspiring musician; serial killer Richard Ramirez was an AC/DC fan; and cannibal Jeffrey Dahmer listened to Iron Maiden. In *Satanism: The Seduction of*

*America's Youth,* Bob Larson cites a young Slayer fan called 'David' who makes pronouncements like: 'I'll murder for the devil. I'm just waiting.'

Characterizing Satan as the personification of totalitarian social control may mask a genuine antipathy toward freedom. In the minds of many, such a powerful authoritarian threat demands authoritarian solutions. Ideologues find in popular music that challenges authority a means of stampeding community leaders, opinion makers, and rank-and-file voters toward authoritarian remedies. The most effective right-wing campaigns exploit real or imagined evidence that the music's content is so far beyond all civilised standards of tolerance that we must dispense with some of our rights in order to vanquish it.

## Jettisoning Freedom of Speech

The first right we are asked to jettison is freedom of speech, which in the USA is inconveniently enshrined within the First Amendment. Theocratic organisations attempt to circumvent the First Amendment in five principal ways:

*Harassment and intimidation directed at artists in an effort to promote self-censorship* These techniques range from anonymous death threats to high-profile lawsuits. In 1985, the parents of a teenage suicide sued Ozzy Osbourne, claiming that his song 'Suicide Solution' drove their son to take his own life. In 1990, the British heavy metal band Judas Priest was sued by parents of another suicide. Although both suits were unsuccessful, they are constantly cited by Christian propagandists seeking to portray the music-suicide link as documented fact.

*Prosecution of artists, retail outlets, broadcasters and record companies* In 1986 Jello Biafra and the Dead Kennedys were charged under California law for disseminating 'material harmful to minors', ostensibly because their album *Frankenchrist* contained HR Giger's poster 'Penis Landscape'. Biafra was acquitted, but the suit helped facilitate the break-up of the band. In 1990, the rap group 2 Live Crew and a record store owner were prosecuted for obscenity in Florida through the efforts of born-again attorney Jack Thompson. Iran-Contra figure Oliver North later retained Thompson as legal advisor in a drive to induce police departments nationwide to indict seditious musicians. These efforts have had limited success in breaching the wall of First Amendment protections, but their effect is chilling.

*Parental advisory labels and ratings* Promoted as an alternative to censorship, such systems have historically been tools of the censors. In the recording industry as well as the film industry, artists are often pres-

> *"Artists are often pressured to drop or change material in order to avoid the stigma of age-restricted status."*

sured to drop or change material in order to avoid the stigma of age-restricted status. In several states, record dealers have been prosecuted for selling 'stickered' albums to minors. Efforts to proscribe all sales of such albums to persons under 18 have recently been defeated in Wisconsin, Tennessee and Georgia. Legal manouevres in Michigan aimed at applying a ratings system to concerts, while thus far unsuccessful, have won widespread support.

*Legislation* Apart from labelling and ratings bills, religious activists have pursued such tactics as an 'obscene live conduct' bill in South Dakota. When such unconstitutional state legislation is signed into law, a protracted and expensive legal challenge may be the only means of overturning it. Recent legislative efforts have targeted the corporations that produce and distribute recordings. In 1997, Governor George W Bush Jr approved a measure prohibiting the state of Texas or any of its agencies from investing in any private concern that owns at least 10 per cent of any corporation that produces music which 'describes, glamorises, or advocates violence, drug abuse or sexual activity'.

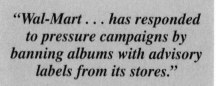

*"Wal-Mart . . . has responded to pressure campaigns by banning albums with advisory labels from its stores."*

*Boycotts* Every issue of the *AFA Journal* contains lists of companies that underwrite the forces Donald Wildmon believes are tearing apart the fabric of society, and offers advice on pressuring them into mending their ways. Triggered by what the AFA calls 'the shameless promotion of homosexuality by Disney/ABC', a boycott of the Walt Disney conglomerate has drawn support from the Catholic League for Religious and Civil Rights, Focus on the Family, the Family Research Council, Concerned Women for America and interdenominational church groups. Disney executives deny that this campaign affects company policy, but early in 1997, shortly after the Southern Baptist Convention joined the boycott, Disney withdrew Insane Clown Posse's *The Great Milenko,* newly released by its subsidiary Island Records and dubbed 'Satanic' by Christian groups, from stores nationwide. Instances of censorship abound at Disney.

## Economic Pressure

The most effective means of encouraging censorship in a profit-driven industry is economic. The recording industry generates US$12 billion annually. As one corporate entity swallows another, small independent labels have become an endangered species, and artists hold diminished power. In this atmosphere, production and sales executives hasten to avoid offence. Wal-Mart, the largest music retailer in the USA, has responded to pressure campaigns by banning albums with advisory labels from its stores, and successfully insisting that producers and musicians provide the 2300 Wal-Mart outlets with censored versions of their product.

The left might once have gone to battle over such restrictive policies. But the American left has recently retreated from traditional commitments to civil liberties, often aiding right-wing attempts to circumscribe speech. The RIAA has been largely ineffectual in its responses, quick to appease, and willing to live with labels and ratings. 'Our side isn't half as organised as the Christian right,' says Parents for Rock and Rap founder Mary Morello. 'There's too much apathy among believers in free speech. Grassroots organisations of fans and musicians like Mass MIC and the Ohio-based Rock Out Censorship have thus far failed to coalesce into a movement, and lack the massive financial backing that fuels the right."

Mass MIC's Nina Crowley notes that few groups have a more sophisticated understanding of the power of money and how to use it than the theocratic right. 'The success of their new strategies will be determined,' she predicts, 'by whether or not the music industry is willing to sell freedom for profit.' Since under US law a corporation is accorded the same First Amendment rights as an individual, the profit option has the blessings of the Constitution. In a society where corporations control all but a dwindling handful of media outlets, and where public space is being engulfed by privatisation, it is fair to question whether or not the First Amendment still has meaning.

# Chapter 3

# Should Pornography Be Censored?

# Chapter Preface

The growth of the Internet in recent years has made a wealth of information available to anyone with a computer and a modem. It has also brought pornography within a few mouse clicks of those who venture into cyberspace—including children. This reality has led many conservative groups and other concerned persons to advocate ways to shield children from exposure to pornographic material on the Net. Solutions include regulations on the transmission of Internet pornography and the use of special software to block pornographic websites in libraries, home computers, and work places. Those who favor such measures believe that pornography is not speech worthy of free speech protection and that therefore regulation is justified. As stated by Barbara Franceski, the director of media for Concerned Women for America, an organization that promotes biblical values,

> These days, the First Amendment to the Constitution is regularly trotted out to justify pornography as a matter of free speech. Our Founding Fathers would be horrified by this interpretation. The First Amendment was designed to protect political speech—not demoralizing filth—in a democracy.

Others insist that efforts to regulate Internet pornography pose serious threats to free speech. For instance, they argue that Internet filtering software, while well meaning, often blocks access to valuable, nonpornographic websites while failing to screen out all of the explicitly pornographic sites. The American Library Association (ALA), the nation's largest professional organization for librarians, is a chief opponent of the use of filtering software in libraries. The ALA states:

> Current blocking/filtering software prevents not only access to what some may consider "objectionable" material, but also blocks information protected by the First Amendment. The result is that legal and useful material will inevitably be blocked. Examples of sites that have been blocked by popular commercial blocking/filtering products include those on breast cancer, AIDS, women's rights, and animal rights.

The ALA and other organizations argue that in order to protect the public's First Amendment rights, alternative means must be found to protect children from the threats posed by on-line pornography, such as increased education and parental involvement. These issues are among the topics discussed in the following chapter.

# Pornography Is Not Protected Speech

## by Frank Morriss

**About the author:** *Frank Morriss is a contributing editor for the* Wanderer, *a weekly Catholic newspaper.*

The logic that views so little as a spanking as child abuse, but defends the "right" to direct obscene or indecent materials at children via online technology, escapes me. If free speech includes the seduction of children, it is time to discuss the basis and rationale for such freedom.

### New Rights for Smut

The truth is that we have arrived at this point of unrestricted expression for public consumption by a process more related to cultural toleration for filth than to genuine development of the law. What would have been considered outside the protection of the common law, national and regional codes of law—and, yes, the U.S. Constitution—as late as a half-century ago, is now found to be a "right" granted by enlightened jurisprudence. Though that is the line of today's judges and jurists, and one found socially and culturally advanced by humanists and so-called progressives (and scatologists, of course), it is in fact hogwash. There is nothing enlightened or progressive, or constitutionally blessed, about inviting linguistic or visual depravity under an umbrella with decent expression. It demeans literature and art to suggest that smut enjoys equal rights with them, and the same is true of even ordinary communication.

### Rewriting the Law

The argument that the distinction between decent and protected communication and the lewd is entirely in the mind of the viewer or the reader is also specious. For centuries, the common taste and presiding judges had little or no trouble in drawing the distinction. If we are to assert the argument (as we should) that the meaning of the Constitution should not be determined by the

Reprinted from Frank Morriss, "The Law Must Return to Its Traditional Sensitivity About Sexual Sewage," *The Wanderer*, August 21, 1997, by permission of the author.

subjective opinions or tastes or proclivities of sitting justices, we should also defend that legal charter against being subject to change by popular tolerations and their expansive character.

But that is precisely what is happening. The law concerning obscenity is being written in conformity to popular acceptance of, and taste for, the lascivious. The pretense is the relativist principle that, as for all things, indecency is defined by the level of toleration or acceptance regarding it. Anything passes for decent in Gomorrah. Any and all sexual practice is ruled normal in Sodom.

## When Nothing Shocks

The seeds of this were contained in judicial reasoning, even in the condemning of obscenity up to World War II, and briefly after it. *Black's Law Dictionary*, drawing from such condemnations, characterizes obscenity forbidden in them as that which offends or shocks. Professor Thomas P. Neill, in his text *The Common Good*, points to abridgment of speech only when it clearly violates "a recognized limit of decency." It follows from these that what does not offend or shock, what is within the understanding of decency, will be considered constitutionally protected. Today, since nothing shocks or offends, and there are no limits set by any understanding of decency, nothing can be judged to be lacking constitutional protection. And that is really what the 1997 Supreme Court decision striking down congressional attempts to protect children from online filth is based upon.

## A New Evangelization

It will take success in a new evangelization to return this nation to an atmosphere in which free sexual expression in words and images is unacceptable. The law would then return to its traditional and reasonable sensitivity about sexual sewage flowing freely in the nation's public communication channels.

Unfortunately, the tendency of religious believers today to accept the prevailing cultural norms, especially in areas of sex, does not give cause for much hope in such an outcome. But if the American people as a

> *"It demeans literature and art to suggest that smut enjoys equal rights with them."*

whole cannot be won over in conscience concerning the unacceptability of openly flaunted pornography, perhaps concern for their children's welfare may work that result.

It is time that scholars, writers, and sociologists researched and presented what sort of society is inevitable if decency in public communication is disregarded. The links between child abuse by pedophiles, child murders by perverts, child prostitution, child kidnapings, and a culture of openly displayed lasciviousness should be established. If all the power of study and investigation can bring about a cultural change regarding smoking because it endangers health, surely similar power should be brought to obscenity because it endangers the safety of those we are bound to protect.

Those aware of that danger should stop being silent or timid because our culture wants to intimidate all and any who would question the decadence and depravity that pass as normal and "liberated." If the dangers of "secondhand" tobacco smoke can cause indignation, it is time we started being indignant about what amounts to "secondhand" abuse, or even rape, of children because there are those, including judges, who think public perversion through communication is somehow entitled to protection.

# Internet Pornography Should Be Restricted

by Nina George Hacker

**About the author:** *Nina George Hacker is assistant editor of* Family Voice, *a monthly magazine published by Concerned Women for America, an organization dedicated to promoting conservative moral values.*

There are more outlets for hard-core pornography in the United States than McDonald's restaurants. Phone sex is now a $6 billion-a-year industry. And an 18-month study by Carnegie Mellon University found over 900,000 sexually explicit displays on the Internet. Is much of this illegal? You bet it is. But why? Isn't porn a matter of free expression, free speech? You might think so, given the way the critics have been raving about the movie, *The People vs. Larry Flynt*—which lionizes the alleged child molester and pornographer who publishes *Hustler* magazine. But there's more to the issue of pornography than Hollywood portrays.

## Free Speech

These days, liberals regularly trot out the First Amendment to the Constitution to justify everything from pictures of men having sex with animals to "snuff" films—in which women are tortured and killed.

Concerned Women for America (CWA) does not believe our Founding Fathers would in any way sanction this interpretation. The First Amendment was designed to protect political speech—not demoralizing filth—in a democratic society.

As long ago as 1712, the Massachusetts Bay Colony criminalized the publication of anything obscene. And in a 1957 review of constitutional history (*Roth v. United States*), the U.S. Supreme Court declared that "obscenity" is not and never has been constitutionally protected "speech."

"A lot of people say that pornography is liberation, that it's all about freedom," noted Concerned Women for America Chairman and Founder, Beverly

Excerpted from Nina George Hacker, "Porn on the Internet: Is It Free Speech?" *Family Voice,* March 1997. Reprinted with permission.

LaHaye. "We say: It's not. In the making of pornography, real victims are forced to undergo humiliation and pain to gratify sick minds."

## Obscene or Just Indecent?

In 1973 (*Miller v. California*), the U.S. Supreme Court established a three-point test for what is illegally obscene. It said that the average person, applying adult community standards, must find that the work in question:

- Appeals to a lewd, abnormal, or degrading interest in nudity, sex, or excretion
- Depicts or describes sexual or excretory acts in an obviously offensive way
- Lacks serious literary, artistic, political, or scientific value

Illegal obscenity is characterized by its graphically explicit portrayal of both normal and perverted sex, including acts involving children. All 50 states have laws against child pornography, and in late 1996, Congress passed the Child Pornography Prevention Act. That law prohibits adults from portraying minors—or even digitally altering photographs—to create pornographic images of children.

> *"The First Amendment was designed to protect political speech—not demoralizing filth."*

There is another class of porn which—however raunchy—is lawful for consenting adults although prohibited for minors. Legal indecency allows sexually arousing "erotica" and semi-nudity. But these materials are not to be displayed publicly, sold to anyone under 18, or broadcast over the airwaves.

## It's Everywhere

Twenty years ago, explicit, deviant or violent pornography was confined to "adult" bookstores and theaters. It could be found in magazines, adult comic books, "peep shows," and X-rated films. Anyone taking part in such things was forced to do so publicly, risking recognition—and shame.

Then came the unprecedented surge of technological advances that gave us videocassettes, pay-per-view cable TV, satellite links, compact disks, and the Internet. All were vehicles for new—private, unaccountable—ways to consume obscenity.

- Surveys revealed that the primary purpose for which most men initially bought a VCR was to view "adult" videos at home.
- Despite a 1989 Supreme Court ruling that obscene phone sex can be banned, U.S. phone companies estimate that dial-a-porn numbers are now receiving half-a-million calls daily.
- According to Attorney Patrick Trueman of the American Family Association, "prosecutable pornography" can be found on "regular cable-TV (Showtime or HBO) two or three nights a week."
- In a recent seven-day period, *Playboy*'s Internet Web site was visited electronically 4.7 million times.

• A new generation of interactive CD-ROMs with titles like "Porno Poker" and "Immoral Combat" allows computer users to strip, photograph, tie up, have sex with—and even mutilate or murder—virtual women in cyberspace.

## Harming America's Families

"People think it's legal," says Kim Gordon, CWA's Legislative Liaison in Iowa. She has been fighting porn in her state. "Their attitude is, 'It's here, people are buying it, so it must be legal.'" And pornographers continue to promote the lie that graphic, perverse, and sexually violent images abound because "consumers want them." If they can successfully claim it is "embraced" by the public, Gordon warns, the purveyors of filth will redefine "community standard"—the key to the Supreme Court's criteria for illegal obscenity.

As more and more illicit sleaze expands into every conceivable medium, why isn't it being prosecuted? With a multi-billion-dollar industry at stake, "pornographers know when they have crossed the line. They do it by design," declares Dr. Jerry R. Kirk, president of the National Coalition for the Protection of Children and Families.

Pat Trueman—chief of the Justice Department's Child Exploitation and Obscenity Section under Presidents Ronald Reagan and George Bush—told *Family Voice:* "Since President Clinton took office, there has been a marked letdown by the Justice Department in prosecuting obscene materials . . . they've appointed very liberal attorneys who don't care about pornography." And, says Kim Gordon, even in cases where obscenity is prosecuted, "the pro-porn lawyers twist 'community standard' until juries are reluctant to convict."

> *"The primary purpose for which most men initially bought a VCR was to view 'adult' videos at home."*

As long as the laws are not enforced, pornography will continue harming America's families. Numerous studies have shown repeatedly that exposure to obscene materials correlates with increased rapes, prostitution, child molestation, violent crime, the abuse of women, and sex addiction in men. Even a surprising number of Christians—including pastors—struggle with pornography and the inappropriate sexual behavior it leads to. Moreover, research has found that 85 percent of the revenue from adult magazines and videos is going into the pockets of organized crime.

## The Ultimate Test Case

Nevertheless, we are seeing an alarming shift in society's acceptance of what Americans once rejected as both immoral and unlawful. With its stigma removed—and support from a permissive legal system—obscenity is filtering into public life as never before. And today's ultimate test case for the "free speech" argument over pornography is the Internet. Across this decentralized, global network, local Internet Service Providers (ISPs), who offer illegal obscenity—and even child pornography—to their customers, are fighting for their "right" to do so.

It began in 1962, with a government proposal for a nationwide system of interconnected defense and military computers that could survive a nuclear attack. Ten years later, electronic mail (e-mail) was established for scientists and educators to exchange information. Then in 1982, technology enabling diverse computer networks to "talk to" each other gave birth to the Internet—with its vast potential for research, communication, entertainment, and business.

Today, nearly 40 million Americans are online—an estimated 4 million are under 18 years old. The four most commonly used "Net" functions are e-mail; access to the World Wide Web; special interest bulletin boards ("newsgroups"); and chat rooms. Obscene pornography can be found on all of them.

America Online, the nation's largest ISP with 8 million subscribers, recently closed down two e-mail accounts that were transmitting child pornography. "Cyberadultery" is becoming more frequent. In 1996, a New Jersey man sued his wife for divorce after discovering her online "affair" conducted entirely by e-mail.

All the major porno magazines have their own "home pages"—displaying both women and men with full frontal nudity, as well as simulated sex acts. In "sex shop" pages, everything from lingerie and condoms, to X-rated videos and vibrators, can be ordered using a credit card. On "personal pages," individuals can post whatever they choose—college boys' favorite pinups; porn stars' self-promotions; or steamy romance fiction and writings on lesbian sadomasochistic practices.

One study found that nearly 85 percent of the images stored on Usenet newsgroups were pornographic. In an electronic search project conducted by *Family Voice*, we were able to quickly and easily access a directory of "sex" sites advertising (among other topics we can't print here): "postings of a prurient nature," bestiality, bondage, "intergenerational sex," masturbation, strip clubs, and voyeurism. In 1996, a Massachusetts man pleaded guilty to charges of raping two teenaged boys he met through a computer bulletin board.

*"Exposure to obscene materials correlates with increased rapes, prostitution, child molestation, . . . and sex addiction in men."*

According to Toronto's Marshall McLuhan Center for Media Sciences, within two years, Internet sex will replace phone sex. Explicit back-and-forth typed conversations describing crude sexual exchanges are commonplace in chat rooms. And deception is rampant. Users often pretend to be of the opposite gender, deny they are married, or fake their age. Worse, pedophiles and homosexuals lurk in chat rooms, luring unsuspecting children into dangerous encounters offline.

In 1995, two schoolteachers were arrested for using the Internet to transmit and receive pictures of children engaging in sex acts. And in July 1996, 13 members of a chat room "club" were charged with using a digital camera to transmit the molestation of a 10-year-old girl as it was happening. They were arrested as part of an on-going FBI investigation into child sexual exploitation on the Net. By late 1996, 80 arrests and 66 felony convictions had been made.

> *"One study found that nearly 85 percent of the images stored on Usenet newsgroups were pornographic."*

*Family Voice* interviewed two Washington, D.C.–area Internet Service Providers [their names have been changed]. We asked them about their policies on pornographic databases. "No one owns the Internet," Bob argued. "It's basically a free-for-all." As such, Bob's company will host any electronic material "as long as it's not illegal." To him, that meant "violation of copyrighted material"—not obscenity—because "pornography is not yet illegal on the Internet."

Dave, whose ISP handles Internet access for two local public school systems, said: "We usually wouldn't refuse anything." His defense? "There is no way to enforce the laws on the Net." Like Bob, Dave was more worried about pirated software than cyberporn.

Dave and others who oppose controls on what is transmitted through cyberspace argue forcefully, "Children can't just stumble across" obscene material. So, *Family Voice* tried an experiment. Using a computer hooked to an ordinary phone line, we logged on to the World Wide Web. We typed in a sex-related word that an average fifth grader has probably heard, either in school or from his friends, and hit "search." In less than 90 seconds, a few clicks of the mouse yielded high-resolution, close-up photos of male genitalia, female breasts, two men kissing, a woman stimulating herself, and a couple engaged in oral sex.

Granted, a warning sign appeared. It stated: "If you are under 18, click on EXIT," not "ENTER." Did the program have a mechanism for stopping a persistent minor? No way!

One newsgroup called "hardcore for amateurs" featured "teaser" photos for "223,545 adult XXX graphic files—raunchier, nastier, dirtier than the rest" and the promise of "1,000 more being added each week!" To go further, an explorer had to click on "join right now for only $10." But what your 10-year-old would have already been exposed to was free. And quickly available to any kid with cyber savvy.

## Something Must Be Done

A fantastic educational tool, the Internet can introduce children to an art museum, help them locate a library book, learn about dinosaurs, or check the weather. But with the same quick clicks of a "mouse," your child can just as easily access pornography. Illegally obscene photographs, stories, and interactive conversations abound—everything from soft-core nudity to homosexual intercourse, child molestation, and graphic images of women being tortured, having sex with animals, and being used as toilets. We protect children from foul influences on city streets. Something must be done to protect them on the "information highway."

In February 1996, Congress passed—and President Clinton signed into law—the Communications Decency Act (CDA). This was the first federal statute to criminalize the distribution of (legal) adult pornography to children via the Internet. It contained an important anti-stalking provision, and would have held ISPs who knowingly carried illegal porn liable. Violators would have risked two years in prison and a $250,000 fine.

But less than 10 days later, 57 plaintiffs—including the American Civil Liberties Union, librarians, and representatives from online services and the communications media—sued in federal court on "First Amendment" grounds. U.S. District Court Judge Ronald L. Buckwalter issued a temporary restraining order; and in June, the Third Circuit Court of Appeals in Philadelphia barred the government from enforcing the CDA. In December 1996, the U.S. Supreme Court voted to review the lower court's ruling. A decision is expected in July 1997. [The U.S. Supreme Court has subsequently declared the CDA unconstitutional.]

> *"Something must be done to protect [children] on the 'information highway.'"*

Prodigy and CompuServe, two of the top four Internet Service Providers, assured *Family Voice* that their sites "in no way contain adult-related, . . . pornographic or sexually explicit information or images." America Online has developed a filter that allows parents to screen Web pages and bulletin boards with sexual or violent content.

In addition, new blocking software such as "Crossing Guard" or "CYBERSitter" is available. "SurfWatch 2.0" censors over 20,000 sites already and offers updates to combat the 800 to 1,000 new "adult" sites the company claims are being added to the Net monthly. A spokeswoman for the Canadian-based Net Nanny told us their software will block "anything [a parent] chooses." But parents should verify that a program works before they allow their children to browse the Net.

## What Parents Can Do

When it comes to monitoring kids in cyberspace, there's no substitute for parental responsibility. Even the best blocking program can be circumvented by a clever youngster.

- Establish firm guidelines for computer use and post them near the terminal.
- Keep the computer out of private areas in your home.
- Spend time with your kids while they are online.
- Instruct children never to disclose personal information.

- Forbid them to arrange any meeting via computer.
- Teach children not to respond to inappropriate communication—and to report it immediately.
- Check out http://www.larrysworld.com/child_safety.html for a safety brochure, or call 800-843-5678 for "Child Safety on the Information Highway"—a free pamphlet available from the National Center for Missing and Exploited Children.
- Share "The Next Right Thing," a comic book from the American Family Association (AFA) that teaches kids how "to make Godly choices when confronted with" obscenity online.

## Activists Respond

Many Christian and pro-family organizations are actively working to stop pornography, both in their local communities and on the worldwide Internet.

On behalf of CWA's 6,000 members in Kentucky, Area Representative Donna Thoreson is fighting to remove two hardcore channels that a cable-TV company inserted into subscribers' services without their consent. CWA of Maryland's AR Conrae Fortlage worked with the Maryland Coalition Against Pornography to hold a Rally for Decency in October 1996. And Kim Gordon and CWA of Iowa helped set up an Obscenity Department in that state's legislature, to prosecute illegal pornography in Iowa.

The American Family Association crusades tirelessly against pornography in the media. Its OutReach program offers counseling help for sex addicts or those struggling with porn—and their spouses. Many churches nationwide take part in the annual "White Ribbons Against Pornography" awareness campaign coordinated by Morality in Media, which also sponsors "Real Men Don't Use Porn" billboards. Enough is Enough! is producing public service ads for network television that will address computer pornography and child safety on the Net.

The Guardian Angels usually monitor America's city streets for crime and danger. Now their "cyber-angels" watch the Net. To date, the Angels told CWA, they have "passed on more than 5,000 pieces of evidence [of illegal cyberporn] to federal authorities."

And in November 1996, a group of Christian leaders—the Religious Alliance Against Pornography—gathered in Washington, D.C., to draft a statement denouncing computer porn.

> *"Obscenity is not a matter of 'free speech,' and should not be allowed, any more than shouting 'fire!' in a crowded theater."*

It reads, in part, "Child pornography and obscenity, which are not protected by the United States Constitution, are evils which must be eliminated."

Concerned Women for America agrees. Pornography violates the dignity of human beings created in God's image and degrades the biblical view of marriage. It leads to devastating consequences for the family and for society. Obscenity is not a matter of "free speech," and should not be allowed, any more than shouting "fire!" in a crowded theater.

"Above all," says Dr. Beverly LaHaye, "this is a spiritual battle." Our first line of defense is prayer. Pray for an end to the distortion of God-given sex within married love. Pray that America will repent for apathetically accepting porn's degradation of men, women, and children. Pray that we will place our children's welfare before the license and greed that masquerade as pornographers' "rights."

# Internet Pornography Should Be Barred from Public Libraries

by Neil Munro

**About the author:** *Neil Munro is a policy reporter for* Washington Technology, *a business newspaper published by the Washington Post Company.*

The American Library Association has an answer for parents who are concerned about pornography on library computers: Buzz off. What's more, the association recommends that libraries furnish private booths in which patrons, including children, may view Internet porn undisturbed. A growing number of protesters—parents, social conservatives, and some librarians themselves—are fighting back.

Their protests stem from the decision of the Supreme Court in June 1996 to void half of the 1996 Communications Decency Act—the half that sought to outlaw the display of online smut to minors. Although the library association, the American Civil Liberties Union, and other groups claim credit for the court's decision, none of them dared challenge the law's other half—the one that bars the display to minors of "obscene" material, the type of porn that fails to meet the legal test of literary, artistic, political, or scientific value. Outside certain business and free-speech enclaves, this law is popular: One poll found that 80 percent of Americans believe government should curb Internet pornography.

## Stocking the Shelves with Porn

This sentiment is shared by most librarians, who have traditionally refused to buy pornographic or otherwise obscene books. Over the last few years, however, more than 40 percent of the nation's libraries have each paid at least $3,000 to buy a computerized portal into the Internet—and so have stocked their electronic shelves with an array of cyberspace porn, complete with color, sound, and full-motion-video action.

Reprinted from Neil Munro, "Quiet in the Library! Children Viewing Porn," *The Weekly Standard*, December 22, 1997, with the permission of *The Weekly Standard*. Copyright, News America, Inc.

The most interesting portion of the Internet is the World Wide Web, which consists of endlessly interlinked series of "Web sites," each containing a storehouse of images and information. To find your way through these millions of pages, you can use any of dozens of electronic indexes, called "search engines." Thus, if you type in "puppy," you will be led to hundreds of Web sites, dedicated to pictures of well-groomed canines, advertisements for pet products, a rock band named Skinny Puppy, a fishing-tackle outfit called Mud Puppy—and a group of deviants at "alt.sex.bestiality," where "Happiness is a warm puppy."

> *"The Internet . . . [converts] computer-equipped libraries— including those in schools— into government-funded peep shows."*

In this way does the Internet provide libraries with instant access to a world of useful information but also convert computer-equipped libraries—including those in schools—into government-funded peep shows. Says Mitzi Brown of the National Law Center for Children and Families in Fairfax, Va., "It is illegal to allow minors into an adult bookstore. Why are we allowing them into the porn sections of the Internet?" Her group advocates restrictions on the Internet links of library computers, contending that the Supreme Court's decision has left online "nonobscene pornography" with even fewer restrictions than porn videos and magazines or *The Simpsons* on television (which is rated TV-PG for bad language).

## Filtering Software

For parents, politicians, and decency-minded librarians, one obvious solution is a type of software that severs libraries' Internet links to offensive Web pages. Naturally, the first generation of this software has had problems, largely because it is difficult to find every pornographic needle in the fast-growing Internet haystack. For example, one product barred access to Web pages containing the words "sex" and "couple," thus blocking a Web page created by the good citizens of Middlesex, England, as well as the White House Web page, which featured the first couple.

This sort of defect has provided ammunition to the library association and allied groups, which call the smut-filtering software "censorware" and argue that developers secretly build into it right-wing political ideology, preventing access to pages that support abortion, homosexuality, or drug use. That objection is being answered by improved technology and trial-and-error experiments. Librarians in Austin, Texas, for instance, have worked with a software developer to narrow the filters to block only obscenity and "gross depictions," while librarians in Boston use very broad filters in the children's corners. The local government in Loudoun County, Va., has voted to install filters in all its computers, while other libraries reject any filter at all, simply keeping their computers near check-out desks, where middle-aged ladies tend to shame the underaged away from porn.

## Opposition to Filters

This jumble of experiments may look like a democratic compromise-in-progress, but the American Library Association will have none of it. Its lobbyists adamantly oppose any and all use of filtering technology and have distributed tip-sheets and legal briefs in support of their cause. According to Judith Krug, director of the association's Office for Intellectual Freedom, any use of smut-filtering software in government-funded libraries is an unconstitutional violation of free-speech rights. In her opinion, no filtering software could be constitutionally valid because no developer can devise a filter that excludes all obscenity while keeping the door open to all less-than-obscene pornography. "Porn is erotica, and that is constitutionally protected speech, and if you don't want your children to access that information, you had better be with your children when they use a computer," she says. And those little booths? They are needed, she maintains, to protect users' privacy. Of parents concerned about Internet porn, Krug is dismissive: "Their number is so small that it is almost laughable." Only one child "out of a trillion billion" might use library computers to seek out porn, she believes.

Krug's touching faith in the virtue of American youth aside, the association's laissez-faire fundamentalism clashes with several facts. First, it is a federal crime to display obscene materials to children. Second, industry is selling cyberspace maps that prod users toward favored Web sites, many of which will soon receive quality rat-

*"It is a federal crime to display obscene materials to children."*

ings. These maps and ratings are prepared by search-engine companies, which make their money by nudging users to corporate Web pages that buy advertising slots or pay for prominent positions in the electronic index. Thus, the association's hands-off approach would, in essence, invite online advertisers to take over the librarians' task of indexing and grading the content of libraries.

## Librarians' Liberal Bias

Third, the association is entirely willing to push kids to certain sites—liberal ones. It has developed a guide to 700 politically correct sites, including those for Young Feminists in NOW, the Sierra Club, multiculturalism, Latin American issues, American Indians, and origami "Cranes for Peace." (There is even one for Louis Farrakhan's Nation of Islam.) Krug says that selecting World Wide Web content is "exactly what librarians are doing, but not in the way [social conservatives] want us to do it."

Her views are entirely representative of the library association's hierarchy. "We don't think we should put blinders on kids," says Barbara Ford, association president. But it is unclear how many of the association's 57,000 members share their leaders' hardline position. Nor is it clear how much of the association's budget comes from the taxpayers, although 36 percent of its $33.8 million in revenue for 1995–96 came from the purchase by libraries of association products. Also, the association's Fund for America's Libraries receives financial support from the National Endowment for the Humanities, the U.S. Information Agency, and the Microsoft Corporation, which seeks to minimize the regulation of its Internet business.

On the smut-filtering issue, the association works hand-in-glove with the American Civil Liberties Union (ACLU). "I don't think [filtering] technology can do the job of a jury and judge" in determining what material meets the legal test of obscenity, says Ann Beeson, an ACLU staff attorney. As for the little booths, she says, "I think that's a good idea." Beeson is threatening to sue libraries that use filters—which is hardly surprising. The ACLU argues that parents should have no right to limit their children's use of library computers, and it backed a California lawsuit that sought to legalize computerized simulations of adult-child sex.

At its base, the argument advanced by the library association and its friends is that the Web should—and will—treat all information equally, undermining traditional morality and promoting "diversity," sexual autonomy, and moral relativism. So far, it seems that they are correct—much to the benefit of corporations, which are delighted to supplant the judgment of librarians with the sell-anything-now ethos of an online marketplace carefully segmented by age, race, wealth, education, and sexual urges.

## Fighting Back

So, what should conservatives do in response? They could adopt a libertarian stance: shut down the libraries and let citizens do their own Web searches at home, with or without filters. Or they could try to take the libraries back from the American Library Association; perhaps local politicians could fire recalcitrant librarians, which would free up cash for computer-equipped charter schools whose librarians treat parents' concerns with respect. The Republican Congress could pass a law that helps parents sue librarians who fail to take reasonable measures to abide by the Communications Decency Act. Congress could even go a step further and prod the Justice Department to jail careless librarians when the computers under their charge are used to break the law.

> *"The ACLU argues that parents should have no right to limit their children's use of library computers."*

There is room for optimism: Several legislators, including Republican senator Dan Coats of Indiana, have drafted bills designed to curb commercial online pornography. Some of the larger Internet companies are eager to buy respectability in suburbia—and protection from porn-related lawsuits brought by outraged parents—by exiling their lucrative online-porn business to backwater reservations in cyberspace, from which filters can bar children. Industry's increased support for filters allows President Bill Clinton and his techno-veep Al Gore to trumpet those filters as "seat-belts for the information superhighway" without worrying about a hostile reaction from Silicon Valley—a reaction that would surely ensue if the Justice Department actually prosecuted online-obscenity cases.

In this debate over technology and morality, conservatives will need a ready-for-TV answer whenever they are slammed as free-speech-hating Babbitts [i.e., conformists]. Judith Krug says of conservatives, "I don't want their view of the world to affect what my kids have access to." Maybe conservatives can simply echo her.

# Filtering Internet Pornography in Libraries Is Not Censorship

## by Roxana Robinson

**About the author:** *Roxana Robinson is the author of the short-story collections* A Glimpse of Scarlet *and* Asking for Love *and the novel* This Is My Daughter.

A 5-year-old is not ready to confront the world. This should be obvious, but it doesn't seem that way to many free-speech advocates, who are angry that some libraries around the country have installed software on their computers to block out Internet material that's unsuitable for children.

The objections are coming from some usual sources: the American Civil Liberties Union, for example, and Web publishers. But even the American Library Association has opposed the use of filtering software.

### The Librarian's Role

Traditionally, the library has been a safe place for children. And librarians have long been the guardians of public virtue. While they have been firm supporters of the First Amendment, they haven't generally interpreted it to mean that they should acquire large holdings of published pornography and make such materials available to children.

Librarians have always acquired books according to their own discrimination and their sense of what is appropriate to their neighborhoods. They generally refuse to buy, among other things, pornography. This isn't censorship; it's common sense.

If a library were to have a section of pornographic books, would we want these to be printed in large, colorfully illustrated, lightweight volumes, shelved near the floor where they were easily available to children? Probably not. But we have gone to a great deal of trouble to insure that computers are user-friendly, with brightly colored graphics and easily accessible information.

Material on the Internet is not only uncensored but also unedited. Adults can be expected to make their own evaluations of what they find. Children, who lack experience and knowledge, cannot.

## False Cries of Censorship

The debate over the filtering of the Internet is a bit like the debate over grants given out by the National Endowment for the Arts. It's all tangled up in false cries of censorship. Censorship is a legal term; it refers to government action prohibiting material from being circulated. This is very different from a situation in which a museum or an arts panel decides not to use public money to finance an exhibition or an artist.

> *"Librarians have always acquired books according to their own discrimination and their sense of what is appropriate to their neighborhoods."*

Commendably, our society defends freedom of speech with great vigor. But there is a difference between allowing everything to be said and allowing everyone to hear it. We should know this by now, having seen the effects that exposure to television and movie violence has on children.

The A.C.L.U. and the American Library Association say that the use of filtering software in computers is censorship because it blocks access to constitutionally protected speech. But these cries are baffling and unfounded. The only control libraries are asserting is over a small portion of the audience, not over the material itself. Moreover, this control has a powerful historical precedent: parental guidance is even older than the Constitution.

The protection of children should be instinctive. A man may have the right to stand on the street and spew obscenities at passers-by, but he would be ordered to leave a kindergarten classroom.

It is absurd to pretend that adults and children are the same audience, and it is shameful to protect the child pornographer instead of the child.

# Government Should Not Censor Pornography

## by Jeffrey J. Douglas

**About the author:** *Jeffrey J. Douglas is a criminal defense attorney and the Executive Director of the Free Speech Coalition, a trade association for the adult entertainment industry.*

*Editor's note: The following viewpoint was originally delivered before the U.S. House of Representatives Subcommittee on Telecommunications, Trade, and Consumer Protection on September 11, 1998.*

Thank you for the opportunity to speak to you as a representative of the adult entertainment industry. . . . I am a criminal defense attorney in Santa Monica, California, and the Executive Director of the Free Speech Coalition, the trade association of the adult entertainment industry.

Established in 1991, the trade association has a two-fold mission. First, to improve the quality of life for the people who create, manufacture, distribute and sell sexually-oriented products and services. The second part of our mission is to improve the external environment for the products and services through education, advocacy, and media and public relations. . . .

## Defining the Terms

The Free Speech Coalition has been very successful in overcoming many of the popular misconceptions regarding sexually oriented entertainment. Typically people and groups hostile to sexuality deliberately interchange terms such as "pornography," "hard core pornography," "violent pornography," "child pornography" and "obscenity." These terms are legally and otherwise distinct.

Through our efforts, the terms of the debate seem to be changing.

Pornography is not a legal term. It is defined by dictionaries as material intended to arouse an erotic response in its audience. That means that an enormous amount of matter, including that which has no sexually explicit content,

Excerpted from Jeffrey J. Douglas's testimony before the U.S. House Committee on Commerce, Subcommittee on Telecommunications, Trade, and Consumer Protection, September 11, 1998.

meets the definition of pornographic, especially including much of the output of Madison Avenue.

"Hard core pornography" or "X-rated" or "Triple X" are also not legal terms.

These are marketing terms, either pejorative or complimentary, depending on the intention of the speaker. Each term is intended to convey to some degree the proportion of sexual images in the material.

## What Adult Entertainment Is Not

"Violent pornography" refers to either non-commercially produced material, or the non-sexually explicit material turned out in large quantities by "mainstream" Hollywood. Rape scenes, mutilations and non-consensual sex scenes are virtually exclusively the province of the non-X-rated genre.

If you want to see a rape scene, you must go to a regular video store like Blockbuster, or watch television. If you patronize an "adult" videostore for such material, you will leave disappointed. For instance, one of the very few categories of sexually explicit material which will be certain to induce an obscenity prosecution is violent or non-consensual material. Thus such material is essentially unknown in the domestic commercial pornography marketplace.

"Child pornography" and "obscenity" refer to materials which are illegal per se.

Even as harsh a critic of the adult entertainment industry as Jan LaRue of the California Law Center for Family and Children, a self-styled anti-pornography advocacy group, testified before the California Legislature that the modern adult entertainment industry is not involved in the production or distribution of child pornography.

Indeed, the Free Speech Coalition, on behalf of the adult entertainment industry, offers a reward of up to $10,000.00 each year for information

> *"If you want to see a rape scene, you must go to a regular video store like Blockbuster, or watch television."*

leading to the arrest and conviction of producers and/or distributors of child pornography.

Part of the goal of the Coalition's educational mission is to remind consumers and legislators alike that pornography is merely another genre of communication. Pornography can contain any kind of representation or content.

## A Diverse Genre

Just like genres such as science fiction, romance, mystery and the like, pornography can be demeaning or empowering of women (or men); it can be reductive or intricate; it can be intellectually complex or crudely raw.

The genre of pornography encompasses the politically and socially conscious materials of Femme Productions (often characterized by their creator Candida Royalle as movies to teach men how to make love to women), to the crudity of the large budget Hollywood star vehicle Silver.

Pornography includes materials which are pedantically educational, as well as purely masturbatory. Use of sexually explicit commercial pornography is now part of the mainstream treatment of options in marriage counseling and psychotherapy. Femme Productions and many similar lines regularly receive letters of appreciation from traditional practitioners such as psychologists, social workers and marriage counselors, praising these videotapes for their contribution to the improved sex lives of their patients.

Additionally, there are explicit materials aimed specifically at non-traditional audiences, such as lines addressing the difficulties of older gay men coming to terms with an unpopular sexual orientation, heavy with storyline and production values. There are explicit stories designed primarily to teach men and women to use condoms and other safer sex techniques. One can no longer make rigid assumptions about the content of sexually explicit materials.

## The Danger of Regulation

The term pornography or the term "adult entertainment" encompasses so much material as to make the terms more confusing than enlightening. And therein lies much of the danger when it comes to regulation.

The regulation of sexually explicit material is most often motivated by the assumption that such material is either harmful to some segment of the population, or of little or no social value. Both these assumptions are false.

As a nation we long ago rejected the notion that materials should be banned based upon the impact such matter might have upon the most vulnerable or easily influenced or traumatized. And for government to engage in censorship practices is violative of the most basic element of the First Amendment.

Let us assume for a moment that most sexually explicit materials were crude, demeaning of the sacred aspects of human sexuality, advocating values inconsistent with the values central to our society, and simply poor-quality communication, but a small percentage were the opposite.

We dare not censor, control or restrict access to all such materials because of the failings of some or even most. Government is uniquely ill-equipped to make determinations as to what is "good" or "high quality" communication. Governmental decisions about communication necessarily will be biased towards non-controversial material.

Furthermore, censorship based upon sexual content will necessarily eliminate the material which makes

> *"For government to engage in censorship practices is violative of the most basic element of the First Amendment."*

serious social contributions, especially if the audience for that material is outside the perceived social mainstream.

Imagine trying to establish guidelines for restricting access to violent images, based upon the assumption that violent imagery encourages actual violence among violence-prone teenagers and young adults. How would one distinguish, on an objective principled basis, between *Texas Chainsaw Massacre* and *Saving Private Ryan*? Or between *A Clockwork Orange* and *Halloween*, Part whatever? Or between an imaginary movie called *The Sexual Deviants of Nazi Medical Experiments* and a different imaginary movie, a serious documentary called *The Victims of Nazi Medical Experiments*?

> **"Government is uniquely ill-equipped to make determinations as to what is 'good' or 'high quality' communication."**

And who should make decisions about restricting access to sexually explicit materials targeted for gay or bi-sexual men and women, people of ethnic backgrounds different from that of the dominant culture, survivors of incest or sexual assaults, to say nothing of materials targeted for non-traditional sexual practitioners, or for people who will never engage in any sexual practices other than the most traditional, but who are curious about divergent sexual practices?

Who should hold the power of the censor for all of the heterogeneous population which we have celebrated for so many generations as representing the diverse strength of this nation? We must trust the audience, the people, to distinguish between good and the bad. That is the essence of the notion of the marketplace of ideas which underlies the intellectual structure of the First Amendment.

# Internet Pornography Should Not Be Censored

by Andrew O'Hehir

**About the author:** *Andrew O'Hehir is a senior editor for* Spin, *a monthly music magazine.*

By the time you read this, the Supreme Court may already have thrown out the Communications Decency Act (CDA), the monumentally ill-advised cyber-censorship law supposedly designed to keep kids from encountering porn on the Internet. [The Supreme Court struck down the CDA in June 1997.] While this particular bad legislation is probably toast, there's a larger lesson not to forget here: People who are frightened by the rapid pace of cultural change will always seek to impose external controls on it, and there will always be callous politicians ready to pander to those frightened people with all kinds of lame, half-baked ideas.

What is worse, some of those politicians—like our endlessly hypocritical President—are willing to support censorship laws they don't really believe in (and know are probably unconstitutional) simply to appease parents' fears about what their kids are seeing and hearing. Bill Clinton signed the CDA in 1996 despite the protests of civil libertarians who pointed out that the law was so poorly drafted it could criminalize not just online porn but discussions of AIDS or breast cancer.

But in April 1997, senior White House aide Ira Magaziner (architect of the fabulously successful national health-care plan from Clinton's first term) said in a speech on electronic commerce that "the administration takes the position that government should not censor content on the Internet." Hello? That would be the same administration that had sent Deputy Solicitor Seth Waxman before the Supreme Court just a few days earlier to argue *in favor* of Internet censorship. There are two possible explanations for this apparent contradiction: either Magaziner's speech—delivered on April Fool's Day—was a Beltway insider's idea of a prank, or the entire Clinton administration is duplicitous slime. You choose.

Reprinted from Andrew O'Hehir, "Indecent Exposure," *Spin*, July 1997, with permission.

*Chapter 3*

## A Tradition of Censorship

Of course, the First Amendment's guarantee of free speech has never stopped generations of moralizing neo-Puritans from trying to censor popular culture in America. For much of the 20th century, the movie industry semi-voluntarily submitted to the restrictions of the Hays Code, which meant that not even married couples could be shown sharing a bed on screen. (Remember Rock Hudson and Doris Day in those twin beds?) The grisly horror comics of the '50s—widely blamed for destroying the moral fiber of youth—gave way to parental outrage and the Comics Code, which mandated "clean" comic books until it was undermined by R. Crumb and his many uninhibited followers. Even in the more refined realm of literature, it took decisions by federal judges before James Joyce's *Ulysses* and D.H. Lawrence's *Lady Chatterley's Lover*, two of the 20th century's most important novels, were allowed into this country.

And that's before we even talk about pop music. From Elvis Presley's pelvic thrusts on *The Ed Sullivan Show* to C. Delores Tucker and William Bennett's efforts to clamp down on gangsta rap, the supposed tribal rhythms and unbridled sexuality of pop have been blamed for every American social ill of the last 40 years. Conservative jurist Robert Bork seems to think the country started down the road to hell with the invention of the transistor radio, which allowed '50s teens to listen to music independent of parental control and influence. As ridiculous as that sounds, he has a point—the portable and inexpensive transistor created a new cultural realm, in much the same way as the Internet has done today.

## Ineffective Measures

The good news is that new cultural realms, by their very nature, can never really be controlled or contained. Today's moral crusaders can't stop techno-savvy young people from exploring every spidery corner of the Web any more than the worried parents of yesteryear could stop kids from listening to the Big Bopper and hiding skin mags under the mattress. More than anything else, the CDA bespeaks politicians' enormous ignorance of how the new media universe works. The law makes it a crime to display "indecent material" to children on the Internet. But it doesn't define what indecency is (although it's a much broader legal concept than obscenity) and offers no clue of how the law is to be enforced.

> *"The First Amendment's guarantee of free speech has never stopped generations of moralizing neo-Puritans from trying to censor popular culture."*

Will SWAT teams descend on the suburban apartments of Web-page designers? Will you have to show your driver's license to buy a computer? Will we all have identity chips implanted in our foreheads so we can't lie about our ages online?

In the end, whatever control measures Congress can cook up for the Internet will be half-assed and ineffective, and any teen Web surfer worth her salt will find the filth without much difficulty. The hunt for porn—in whatever medium it presents itself—is a key ritual of adolescence, just as the attempt to hide all frank discussion of sexuality from adolescents is a key ritual of bourgeois adulthood. Civil-liberties attorney Bruce J. Ennis, Jr., in arguing against the CDA before the Supreme Court, told the justices that "government cannot constitutionally reduce the adult population to reading and viewing only what is appropriate for children." That's true, of course. It's also true that government—short of a Christian Coalition coup—will never find a way to stop "children" from reading and viewing what is allegedly for adults. And that's as it should be.

> *"Today's moral crusaders can't stop techno-savvy young people from exploring every spidery corner of the Web."*

# Libraries Should Not Filter Internet Pornography

## by Internet Free Expression Alliance

**About the author:** *The Internet Free Expression Alliance is a group of organizations committed to protecting free speech on the Internet.*

*Editor's note: This viewpoint was excerpted from a statement submitted to the National Commission on Library and Information Science on December 14, 1998.*

Undeniably, the Internet provides access to knowledge and expression in ways never before possible. It is a venue where "any person can become a town crier with a voice that resonates farther than it could from any soapbox," as the U.S. Supreme Court observed in 1997 in its landmark decision in *Reno v. ACLU*. From remote learning classes to digital art museums to library collections and news from all over the world, Internet technologies provide an essential tool for learning and communication.

## Exaggerated Claims

Recognizing the increased use and access provided by public libraries, the Commission has stated that it is holding this inquiry on use of the Internet in libraries to produce a report containing recommendations to assist library managers in addressing problems arising from public access Internet terminals in libraries where children may use them. The Commission has stated that "foremost of these problems is the potential for predation by pedophiles," and that its report will also deal with the concerns of parents about their children having access to inappropriate material, and privacy issues surrounding direct marketing efforts targeted at minors. We applaud the Commission for conducting this inquiry and believe that promoting safe and effective use of online resources is a laudable objective. We submit these comments not only to offer suggestions on protecting children's safety and privacy online, but also to put this debate in proper perspective and to avoid over-emphasis on exaggerated claims of abuse of online information. For example, we are not convinced that

Excerpted from the Internet Free Expression Alliance, "Kids and the Internet: The Promise and the Perils," joint statement for the record submitted to the National Commission on Library and Information Science, December 14, 1998.

there is any correlation between library Internet access and predation by pe-dophiles. Sexual abuse of children, child pornography and obscenity are all ille-gal—online and offline—and are not constitutionally protected. In addition, ex-isting laws prohibiting the dissemination of these materials are being enforced aggressively in cyberspace.

Moreover, we caution the Commis-sion against drawing the conclusion that the online availability of consti-tutionally protected speech that some people find objectionable mandates the adoption of restrictive methods

> *"We are not convinced that there is any correlation between library Internet access and predation by pedophiles."*

that contravene First Amendment principles. Indeed, the recent court decision in *Mainstream Loudoun v. Loudoun County Library Board*, holding that a li-brary policy mandating the use of filtering software in all library terminals was unconstitutional, underscores the importance of not rushing to embrace overly restrictive solutions. The *Mainstream Loudoun* opinion (written by a judge who is a former librarian) found little or no evidence that there are any harms pre-sented by providing unfiltered access to constitutionally protected material in public libraries. The decision states, in pertinent part:

> The only evidence to which defendant can point in support of its argument that the Policy is necessary consists of a record of a single complaint arising from Internet use in another Virginia library and reports of isolated incidents in three other libraries across the country. In the Bedford County Central Public Library in Bedford County, Virginia, a patron complained that she had ob-served a boy viewing what she believed were pornographic pictures on the In-ternet. This incident was the only one defendant discovered within Virginia and the only one in the 16 months in which the Bedford County public library system had offered unfiltered public access to the Internet. After the incident, the library merely installed privacy screens on its Internet terminals which, ac-cording to the librarian, "work great."

> The only other evidence of problems arising from unfiltered Internet access is described by David Burt, defendant's expert, who was only able to find three libraries that allegedly had experienced such problems, one in Los Angeles County, another in Orange County, Florida, and one in Austin, Texas. There is no evidence in the record establishing that any other libraries have encoun-tered problems: rather, Burt's own statements indicate that such problems are practically nonexistent. Significantly, defendant has not pointed to a single in-cident in which a library employee or patron has complained that material be-ing accessed on the Internet was harassing or created a hostile environment. As a matter of law, we find this evidence insufficient to sustain defendant's burden of showing that the Policy is reasonably necessary. No reasonable trier of fact could conclude that three isolated incidents nationally, one very minor isolated incident in Virginia, no evidence whatsoever of problems in Loudoun County, and not a single employee complaint from anywhere in the country

establish that the Policy is necessary to prevent sexual harassment or access to obscenity or child pornography.

## Guidance for Libraries

In finding the Loudoun County mandatory filtering policy unconstitutional, the court provided important guidance that should be a starting point for the Commission in making recommendations about how best to provide guidance on Internet use in libraries. The court noted that:

- Libraries must consider the First Amendment in making content decisions;
- Mandatory blocking constitutes "prior restraint"—an extreme form of censorship that few courts have allowed;
- Any library policy that censors adults in the guise of protecting minors is unconstitutional;
- Alternatives to blocking software, even those that are less restrictive, are not necessarily constitutional.

In submitting this statement, we therefore seek to ensure that the Commission does not unnecessarily limit the vibrancy and openness of the Internet as a communication medium by embracing standards or techniques, such as blocking and filtering technologies, that may provide some members of the public with a false sense of security, while blocking access to valuable content.

Our testimony outlines:

I. Reasons why libraries provide such a crucial access point for many segments of our population, especially the poor, and why that means that providing unfiltered access is so important.

> *"Blocking and filtering software programs cannot possibly filter out all objectionable material."*

II. Why educational information and programs are both better from a public policy perspective and are constitutionally sound.

III. Why blocking and filtering programs remove decision-making authority about material selection from librarians and parents.

IV. Why blocking software under-blocks speech that some may find objectionable while blocking valuable and constitutionally protected speech.

V. Finally, we provide a section that includes suggestions for less restrictive alternatives that may better address concerns about privacy and safety online.

We conclude that blocking and filtering software programs cannot possibly filter out all objectionable material and instead may provide communities with a false sense of security about providing access. We believe that no filter can offer the protections provided by education and training.

## The "Digital Divide"

*I. Libraries provide the only access to the Internet for many individuals*

While Internet communications are increasingly recognized as dynamic

learning vehicles, it is also true that the gap between Americans with access—
either in their homes or libraries—and those without such access, has widened.
A recent report by the National Telecommunications Information Administration, "Falling Through the Net II: New Data on the Digital Divide," found that:

> [d]espite th[e] significant growth in computer ownership and usage overall,
> the growth has occurred to a greater extent within some income levels, demo-
> graphic groups, and geographic areas, than in others. In fact, the "digital di-
> vide" between certain groups of Americans has increased between 1994 and
> 1997 so that there is now an even greater disparity in penetration levels among
> some groups. There is a widening gap, for example, between those at upper
> and lower income levels. . . .

Just as libraries have always been great equalizers, providing books and other
information resources to help people of all ages and backgrounds live, learn
and work, today libraries provide critical access to the wealth of information in
the digital world. Indeed, the NTIA concluded that libraries and other community access centers will play a vital role in connecting many computer "have
nots" until it is possible to make universal service for all households a reality.
This finding has also been supported by a recent American Library Association
and National Commission on Libraries and Information Sciences survey that
found that one in five public libraries serve populations with a poverty level of
20 percent or more and one in ten serve rural areas with greater than 20 percent
poverty level. Thus, safeguarding Internet access provided by libraries is an extremely important objective, not only because libraries have traditionally
served as a forum for expressive activity, but because today they serve as the
only access point to the vast world of online resources for large segments of
our population.

## Guidance and Education

*II. Educating users, not blocking speech, is sound and effective public policy*

In 1997, the Supreme Court struck down the Communications Decency Act
("CDA"), which would have made it a crime to communicate "indecent" materials on the Internet. The Court
found that the CDA violated the First
Amendment and indicated that "the
interest in encouraging freedom of
expression in a democratic society
outweighs any theoretical but un-
proven benefit of censorship." In its
historic decision, the Supreme Court
recognized that the Internet, as much

> *"Filtering software . . . does
> not only block material that
> is legally obscene or
> 'inappropriate' for minors;
> it blocks a much wider
> spectrum of speech."*

as books and newspapers found in our public libraries, is entitled to the very
highest level of First Amendment protection. While the Internet provides access to material that some parents and educators may find objectionable, pro-

tecting children's safety should not be equated with the use of filtering software in public libraries. The use of filtering software is simply inconsistent with constitutional mandates and good public policy, as it does not only block material that is legally obscene or "inappropriate" for minors; it blocks a much wider spectrum of speech and is simply incapable of discerning between constitutionally protected and unprotected speech.

> *"No filtering software can replace the importance of teaching children not to post personally identifiable information online."*

Clumsy and ineffective blocking programs are "quick fix" solutions to parental concerns. They provide a false sense of security that minors will be protected from all material that some parents may find inappropriate. At the same time, filtering software restricts access to valuable, constitutionally protected online speech about topics ranging from safe sex, AIDS, gay and lesbian issues, news articles, and women's rights. Religious groups such as the Society of Friends and the Glide United Methodist Church have had online resources blocked by these imperfect censorship tools, as have policy groups like the American Family Association. This type of arbitrary censorship, when used in public libraries, is a blatant violation of the First Amendment.

Instead, parents and educators should be fully informed about the responsibilities they must shoulder and the potential abuses of which they should be aware. No software or restriction on content can fulfill those goals, but education of parents, of students and of educators and librarians can give them all the tools to provide appropriate safeguards. We believe that:

- No filtering software can replace the importance of teaching children not to post personally identifiable information online. Proper guidance and education can.
- No filtering software can teach a user how to evaluate the accuracy of information online. Proper guidance and education can.
- No filtering software can promote responsibility against abusing online information or the privilege of access. Proper guidance and education can.

To promote user safety and responsibility, we have provided a suggestions section in the final section of this statement that offers concrete steps that libraries may take to foster safe and effective use of online resources. The following section provides further detailed findings on the problems relating to the use of filters and blocking software in libraries.

## Letting Vendors Decide

*III. Blocking and filtering programs remove decision-making authority from educators and librarians*

In order to block Internet sites, a software vendor identifies categories of material to be restricted and then configures its software to block sites containing those categories of speech. Using its criteria, the software vendor compiles and maintains lists of "unacceptable" sites. Some software blocking vendors employ individuals who browse the Internet for sites to block, while others use automated searching tools to identify which sites to block. Some do both. However, all blocking software requires the exercise of subjective human judgment by the vendor to decide what speech is acceptable and what is unacceptable.

Blocking software providers generally do not disclose their lists of unacceptable sites because they regard the lists as proprietary. As a result, it is impossible for parents, educators and librarians to make decisions about what sites should be blocked, and what content should be available. Many of these programs do not even provide users with the ability to unblock sites that are inappropriately restricted.

Hence, using blocking programs means that librarians do not have the direct authority to determine what matter is "inappropriate for minors," and they may be virtually powerless to make this determination. Librarians do not participate in the original selection of material that is deemed "inappropriate," and cannot easily unblock restricted material. Such determinations are made by the software vendor, who regards the product of its determinations a trade secret that cannot be disclosed to anybody, including the affected library.

> *"The use of [filtering] programs eliminates the essential role of parents, librarians, and teachers."*

Public libraries' use of filtering software is fundamentally inconsistent with the role of the library as a storehouse of information. The use of such programs eliminates the essential role of parents, librarians, and teachers and places decision-making into the hands of commercial software vendors. The American Library Association has opposed the use of filters in libraries because it recognizes that it is the domain of parents not librarians, the government, or faceless software companies to oversee the use of the library by their children. See Resolution adopted by ALA Council, July 2, 1997.

## Removing Books from the Shelves

For these reasons, free speech groups (including the American Civil Liberties Union and a grassroots civil liberties organization, Mainstream Loudoun) challenged the decision of the Loudoun County, Virginia, Library Board to implement a policy that required the use of blocking software at all library computer terminals. The library's Internet policy purported to require the blocking of access to materials that are "pornographic" or "harmful to juveniles." However, what the plaintiffs found was that the software chosen by the Loudoun libraries blocked far more than this vague category of speech. The ACLU, which represented website and content providers in the suit, charged that the following sites were among those that were blocked by the filtering program:

The Safer Sex Page, operated by Chris Filkins;

Banned Books Online, created by John Ockerbloom;

American Association of University Women Maryland (AAUW Maryland);

Rob Morse, an award-winning columnist for the *San Francisco Examiner*;

Books for Gay and Lesbian Teens Youth Page, created by 18-year-old Jeremy Myers;

Sergio Arau, the popular Mexican artist and rock singer known as "El Padrino";

Renaissance Transgender Association, a group serving the transgendered community;

The Ethical Spectacle, created by author Jonathan Wallace.

The court therefore found that by using blocking software to implement the policy, the library board's action was the digital equivalent of "removing books from the shelves" of the library in violation of the Constitution, even though the affected speech has value to both adults and minors. At the same time, the judge cited the experience of other Virginia librarians in suggesting that Loudoun County could use a variety of less restrictive means to keep children from accessing inappropriate material online.

## Blocking Access to Information

*IV. Blocking software restricts access to valuable, protected speech*

The use of blocking programs on library terminals used by students is also problematic because it may limit their ability to complete homework or research assignments on a variety of subjects ranging from sexual harassment, abortion and medical issues, to artwork and literature. In 1998, a California library that removed filtering software after public disapproval conceded that the filters presented an unconstitutional barrier to patrons seeking access to materials including legal opinions, medical information, political commentary, art, literature, information from women's organizations, and even portions of the American Civil Liberties Union's Freedom Network page on the World Wide Web.

The huge size of the Web makes it impossible for any individual to review all sites or to keep up with the exponential number of new sites that come online and change daily. Thus, developers of blocking software must rely on automated search tools to identify sites to block. These tools cannot block according to subject matter, and cannot evaluate pictures. They can only identify sites by searching for a particular word or string of words. As a result, these tools inevitably identify sites that do not contain the subject matter the producers of the software want to block.

*"The use of blocking programs on library terminals used by students . . . may limit their ability to complete homework or research assignments."*

This result is not surprising. Several reports compiled by educators, public interest organizations, and other interested groups have concluded that filtering software inappropriately blocks valuable, protected speech, and does not effectively block many of the sites they are intended to block.

One report, by the Electronic Privacy Information Center (EPIC), "Faulty Filters: How Content Filters Block Access to Kid-Friendly Information on the Internet," found that filtered search engines reduced access to constitutionally protected and valuable content available on the World

> *"Students should be taught to develop critical thinking skills when using the Internet."*

Wide Web. The EPIC Report reviewed the impact on Internet access of "Family Search," a "family-friendly search engine" from the Net Shepherd firm. The EPIC Report compared the search results received from 100 Internet search inquiries using the popular search engine AltaVista to the search results received when the results for the same 100 searches were filtered through Family Search. The search terms included topics that students might be likely to research, such as "American Red Cross," "Thomas Edison" and "Bill of Rights." It concluded that the "family-friendly search engine . . . typically blocked access to 95–99 percent of the material available on the Internet that might be of interest to young people." The report also determined that the search engine did not seem to restrict access to topics regarded as sensitive with respect to young people any more than it restricted access to matters of general interest.

Many other public interest groups and news organizations have reported similar findings. . . .

As these reports and news articles demonstrate, use of filtering programs by public institutions can result in discrimination against speakers based on their viewpoints, and can restrict access to a variety of constitutionally protected and important speech, even as to minors.

## Education and Use Policies

*V. More effective measures for promoting safety exist*

Parents should be informed that the blind reliance on filtering and blocking programs cannot effectively safeguard children from "inappropriate" material. They should be made aware of the studies that show that blocking software may allow access to material that some parents believe is objectionable while restricting access to otherwise innocuous or educational speech.

We further suggest that:

• Acceptable use policies should be developed. Many libraries have developed carefully worded acceptable use policies that provide instructions for parents, teachers, students, librarians and patrons on use of the Internet. Such policies may include content-neutral time limits as to when and how young people should use the Internet. These policies can be enhanced by encouraging instruction for parents, teachers, students, librarians and patrons on use of the Internet.

• "Driver's Ed" programs for Internet users should be offered. Students should be taught to develop critical thinking skills when using the Internet and to be careful about relying on inaccurate resources online. One way to teach these skills in schools is to condition Internet access for minors on successful completion of a seminar similar to a driver's education course. Such seminars could emphasize the dangers of disclosing personally identifiable information such as one's address, communicating with strangers about one's personal life or about intimate matters, or relying on inaccurate resources on the Internet. Such programs can also teach users how to best perform searches to obtain the relevant information that they seek. . . .

• Users should be encouraged to use recommended links and sites. Libraries and schools should publicize and provide links to websites that have been recommended for children and teens. A wide variety of websites, pamphlets, and books provide lists of child-appropriate content. In addition, some filtering software includes lists of suggested sites for children to explore. Examples of suggestion mechanisms include: Yahooligans!, Bonus.com, The Internet Kids & Family Yellow Pages, and Scholastic Network. . . .

• Use of privacy screens should be encouraged. To avoid unwanted viewing of websites by passers-by—and to protect users' privacy when viewing sensitive information—libraries and schools should place privacy screens around Internet access terminals in a way that minimizes public view.

• Finally, some libraries have offered blocking software as a voluntary option for patrons who wish to use it.

## An Immutable Ideal

The advent of new forms of communication technology is always a cause for public anxiety and unease. This was as true for the printing press and the telephone as it was for the radio and the television. But the constitutional ideal is immutable regardless of the medium: a free society is based on the principle that each and every individual has the right to decide what kind of information he or she wants—or does not want—to receive or create.

We encourage the Commission to further take the lead in fostering a discussion that will help local communities find the best answers to providing greater access to the Internet. Members of the Internet Free Expression Alliance and the Free Expression Network have concluded that blocking and filtering software programs cannot possibly filter out all objectionable material and instead may provide communities with a false sense of security about providing access. We believe that no filter can offer the protections provided by education and training. Thus, we believe that the importance of user education should not be underestimated as a critical tool for teaching safe, responsible, and rewarding use of cyber-communications and encourage the Commission to encourage an educational approach.

# Internet Filtering Software Threatens Free Speech

by Joshua Micah Marshall

**About the author:** *Joshua Micah Marshall is a freelance writer and the editor of a monthly newsletter on Internet law.*

When the Supreme Court overturned the Communications Decency Act (CDA) in the summer of 1997, its decision seemed to put to rest much of the controversy over Internet free speech. But there are now a host of more limited efforts afoot to prune back the range of Internet content and limit access to various kinds of on-line material. Such technical innovations as "content filtering" and "censor-ware" make it possible for individuals, employers, Internet service providers, and others to block out selected portions of the online world. While the CDA's criminal penalties for publishing "indecent" material made an easy mark for free speech advocates, these new forms of control pose more subtle and incremental threats—and should force us to confront whether keeping the government out of the censorship business will be sufficient to assure freedom online.

The new world of online media is inevitably changing the terms of debate about freedom of speech and of the press. Words, ideas, and images are being liberated from their original connection to such physical objects as books, papers, magazines, and photographs, and the costs of copying and transmitting information are dropping sharply. Just what constitutes "publishing," for instance, becomes blurred when books, articles, and even casual notes can be distributed to the entire world, instantaneously and at negligible cost. Much of the difficulty of crafting good public policy for the Internet stems from the fact that the Net removes all the incidental and often overlooked ways in which we have traditionally used physical space to segregate and restrict information. Consider the fact that *Playboy* magazine is behind the counter and not on the magazine rack at the local convenience store, or that certain subterranean activities can only be found in the seedier sections of our central cities. If these tacit ways of organizing information are to be reproduced on the Internet, they must be explicitly reconstituted. But often these barriers can only be rebuilt with meddlesome and obtrusive changes in the way the Web works.

## The PICS Is In

Much of the debate over how to reconstitute the old barriers and regulate the flow of online information centers on "content filtering" and something called PICS (the Platform for Internet Content Selection). PICS originated in the minds of the men and women who designed the World Wide Web. While Congress was hashing out what would become the Communications Decency Act, a group of Internet policy planners began to formulate a system that would allow individual users to decide what could and could not appear on their computer screens. Rather than banning information at the "sending" end, Internet users would be able to block offensive material at the "receiving" end. Everybody could then carve out his or her own zone of comfort on the Internet, with just the right mix of Puritanism and prurience. It was an ingenious solution—a kinder, gentler version of the CDA. It would assuage the fears of parents, conciliate free speech advocates, and short-circuit the political argument for a broad regime of Internet censorship.

The PICS project was coordinated and directed through the World Wide Web Consortium, an independent body that has taken a leading role in formalizing standards and protocols for the Web, with support from many of the biggest Internet industry companies. The designers went to great lengths to make the system unobjectionable to both civil libertarians and those who wanted to limit the circulation of indecent material. In fact, their literature betrays an almost quaint sensitivity to the theory and language of multiculturalism. They designed PICS not as a set of ratings or categories but as a format for devising a variety of different ratings systems, each reflecting different cultural and political perspectives. To understand the distinction, consider the difference between a word processing format like Microsoft Word and the infinite variety of documents that one could author in that format. PICS is not a rating system; it is a format that can be used to create many different rating systems.

> *"The new world of online media is inevitably changing the terms of debate about freedom of speech and of the press."*

PICS envisions at least two basic models in which rating systems might operate. The first—and conceptually more straightforward—is self-rating. Publishers of Web sites rate their own material, alerting viewers to coarse language, nudity, or violence. Publishers would choose whether to rate their sites and, if so, what ratings system to use. PICS would also allow third-party rating. Different organizations or companies could set up "rating bureaus" that would rate sites according to their own political, cultural, or moral standards. Thus the Christian Coalition might set up its own rating bureau, as could the National Organization for Women. Individual users could then decide whether to filter material using the voluntary self-ratings or subscribe to a rating bureau that suited their personal sensibilities.

## Upstream Filtering

Given the obvious similarities, many have compared PICS to an Internet version of the much-touted V-chip. But the V-chip analogy is only partly correct, and the differences are telling. The weight of the argument for the content filtering approach is that individuals decide what they will and will not see. But PICS-based content filtering is actually much more flexible and scalable than this standard description implies. There are many links in the information food chain separating your personal computer from the source of information. And what you see on the Internet can potentially be filtered at any of those intermediate points. You can block material at your computer, but so can libraries, your employer, your Internet service provider, your university, or even—depending on where you live—your nation-state. With the V-chip you control what comes on your television set. But with PICS the choice may not be yours.

> *"There are many links in the information food chain. . . . And what you see on the Internet can potentially be filtered at any of those intermediate points."*

There are already a host of new software products on the market that allow this sort of "upstream" content filtering. They are being introduced widely in the workplace and, to a lesser degree, in schools and libraries. This so-called Internet access management software makes possible not just filtering and blocking but also detailed monitoring of Internet usage. It can monitor what *individual* users view on the Web and how long they view it. It can even compile percentages and ratios of how much viewing is work related, how much is superfluous, and how much is simply inappropriate. These less savory uses of the technology won't necessarily be used. But the opportunities for abuse are obvious and they reach far beyond issues of free speech into elemental questions of personal privacy.

The other problem with PICS is more subtle and insidious. You often do not know just what you are not seeing. Because of a perverse but seemingly inevitable logic, companies that provide content filtering or site blocking services must keep their lists hidden away as trade secrets. The logic is clear enough. The companies expend great resources rating and compiling lists of prohibited sites; to make those lists public would divest them of all their value. But whatever the rationale, this practice leads to numerous tangled situations. Public libraries that have installed site blocking software are in the position of allowing private companies to determine what can and cannot be viewed in the library. Even the librarians don't know what is blocked and what is not.

## Becoming Invisible

The possible integration of search engine technology and PICS-based rating holds out the prospect of a Web where much of the material that would not appear on prime-time television just slips quietly out of view. Even more unsettling, many Internet search engine companies—with a good deal of prodding from the White House—have announced plans to begin refusing to list sites that will not, or cannot, rate themselves. Again, the implications are far-reaching. With the increasing size and scope of material on the Web, most people use search engines as their gateway to finding information online. Not being listed is akin to having the phone company tell you that you are welcome to have as many phone numbers as you like but no listings in the phone book. This is one of the ways in which "voluntary" self-rating can quickly become a good deal less than voluntary. There are also bills pending before Congress that would either mandate self-rating or threaten sanctions for "mis-rating" Internet content. This is the sort of creeping, indirect censorship that makes PICS so troubling.

One of the compensations of real-world censorship is that school boards and city councils actually have to ban unpopular books and look like fools doing it. The crudeness and heavy-handedness of the state's power to censor is always one of the civil libertarians' greatest advantages in battles over the banning and burning of books. But content filtering makes censorship quiet, unobtrusive, and thus all the more difficult to detect or counter. It is difficult to quantify just what is different about the new information technology. But the essence of it is an increasing ability to regulate the channels over which we communicate with one another and find out new information.

To all these criticisms the creators of PICS say simply that they and their technology are neutral. But this sort of "Hey, I just make the guns" attitude is hardly sufficient. To their credit, they also point to the more positive uses of content filtering. And here they have a point. In its current form the Internet is a tangled jumble of the useful, the useless, and the moronic. PICS could help users cut through the clutter. Topic searches could become more efficient. In one oft-cited example, content filtering could allow Internet searches for information about a particular medical condition that would produce only material from accredited medical organizations. Of course, the question then becomes, who accredits? There are standards of authority and discrimination we will gladly accept

> *"Content filtering makes censorship quiet, unobtrusive, and thus all the more difficult to detect or counter."*

about information for treating breast cancer that we would never accept if the topic is, say, art or political speech. And in any case none of these potentially positive uses negates, or really even speaks to, the reality of possible abuses.

This new debate over content filtering has sliced apart the once potent coalition of interests that banded together to defeat the Communications Decency

Act. One of the striking features of the anti-CDA fight was how it lined up technologists, civil libertarians, and major corporations on the same side. What became clear in the aftermath, however, was that companies like Microsoft, Netscape, and IBM were not so much interested in free speech, as such, as they were in preventing government regulation—two very distinct concepts that we now tend too often to conflate.

In fact, the seamless and adaptable censoring that makes civil libertarians shudder is precisely what makes it so attractive to business. Businesses do not want to refight culture wars in every locale where they want to expand Internet commerce. If parents from the Bible Belt are afraid that their children will find gay rights literature on the Web, they won't let them online to buy Nintendo game cartridges either. The same logic is even more persuasive when commerce crosses international borders. International Internet commerce is widely seen as one of the most lucrative prospects for the Internet industry, and much of that trade would take place with countries that either do not share American standards of cultural permissiveness or that routinely censor political material. Content filtering will let American companies sell goods to China over the Internet without having to worry that pro–Tibetan independence Web sites will sour the Chinese on the Internet altogether. Content filtering allows us to carve the Internet up into countless gated communities of the mind.

> *"The seamless and adaptable censoring that makes civil libertarians shudder is precisely what makes it so attractive to business."*

These concerns about "cyber-rights" can seem like overwrought digital chic—an activism for the affluent. And often enough, that is just what they are. But it is important to take a broader view. Today the Internet remains for most a weekend or evening diversion and only relatively few of us use it intensively in the workplace. But the technologies and principles that we formulate now will ripple into a future when the Internet—and its successor technologies—will be more and more tightly stitched into the fabric of everyday communication. In a world of books and print, the "Government shall make no law" formulation may be adequate. But in a world of digitized information, private power to censor may be just as deleterious as public power, and in many respects may be more so.

## Free Expression at Risk

There is also an unfortunate convergence between this growing power of nongovernmental censorship and the declining value of open expression as a positive social ideal. In a political climate such as ours, which is generally hostile to government power, a subtle and perverse shift can take place in our understanding of the First Amendment and the importance of free speech. We can begin to identify the meaning of free speech simply as a restriction on governmental power and lose any sense that free speech has value on its own merits. One might say that it is the difference between free speech and free expression, the former being narrow and juridical, based largely on restrictions on government action, and the latter being a more positive belief not in the right but in the value of open expression for its own sake. We seem to be moving toward a public philosophy in which we would shudder at the thought of government censoring a particular

> *"There is no easy translation of real-world standards of intellectual freedom into the online world."*

book or idea but would be more than happy if major publishing companies colluded together to prevent the same book's publication.

Our political and cultural landscape is replete with examples. We see it in support for the V-chip, government's strong-arming of TV networks to adopt "voluntary" ratings, and in the increasingly fashionable tendency for political figures to shame entertainment companies into censoring themselves. The sort of public shaming of which Bill Bennett has made a career has a very good name in our society, and too few speak up against it. The move to rate television programming may well be benign or, at worst, innocuous in itself. But it points to a broader trend for government to privatize or outsource its powers of censorship. This sort of industry self-regulation is said to be voluntary. But more and more often it is "voluntary" in the sense that Senator John McCain must have had in mind when he threatened to have the Federal Communications Commission consider revoking the broadcasting licenses of NBC affiliates if the network did not agree to adopt the new "voluntary" TV rating system.

The idea that there will be a great multiplicity of rating systems may also be deceptive. Despite the possibility of an infinite variety of rating systems for a multitude of different cultural perspectives, everything we know about the computer and Internet industries tells us that pressures lead not toward multiplicity but toward concentration. Aside from Microsoft's various anticompetitive practices, basic structural forces in the computer and software industries make it likely that we will have one or two dominant operating systems rather than five or six. The Web browser market has followed a similar trend toward consolidation. There would likely be a greater demand for a diversity of options in the market for content filtering and site blocking services. But the larger, overarching economic pressures—and the need to create vast economies of scale—would be simply overwhelming. Effectively rating even a minute portion of the Web would be an immense undertaking. The resources required to rate the Web and constantly update those ratings could be recouped only by signing up legions of subscribers. Far more likely than the "let a hundred flowers bloom" scenario is one in which there would be a few large companies providing content filtering and site blocking services. And these would be exactly the kind of companies that would become the targets of crusading "family values" politicians trying to add new candidates to the list of material to be blocked.

## The First Amendment, Updated

The novelty of this new information technology calls on us to think and act anew. We cannot now foresee what changes in technology are coming or what unexpected implications they will have. What is clear, however, is that there is no easy translation of real-world standards of intellectual freedom into the online world. Our current conceptions of First Amendment rights are simply unequal to the task. It is easy enough to say that the First Amendment should apply to cyberspace, but crude applications of our current doctrines to the online world involve us in unexpected and dramatic expansions and contractions of intellectual freedoms and free speech. In the architecture of the new information economy, private power will have a much greater and more nimble ability to regulate and constrict the flow of information than state power will. Taking account of this will mean updating both the jurisprudence and the public philosophy of free speech rights. Much like the law of intellectual property, public policy toward free speech must undertake a basic reconsideration of the values it seeks to protect and the goals it seeks to serve.

Partly this will mean focusing more on the goals of First Amendment freedoms and less on the specific and narrow mechanics of preventing government regulation of speech. It may even mean considering some informational equivalent of antitrust legislation—a body of law that would intervene, not to regulate the content, but to ensure that no private entity or single corporation gained too great a degree of control over the free flow of information. What it certainly does mean is that we must abandon that drift in public policy that allows government to outsource its power to censor under the guise of encouraging industry self-regulation. Government may not be fully able to alter some of the pernicious directions in which information technology is evolving—and it may be good that it cannot. But government can at least avoid policies that reinforce the negative tendencies. "Voluntary" industry self-regulation should really be voluntary and we should inculcate within ourselves—and particularly our policymakers—a critical awareness of the implications of new technologies. Whatever the merits of creating PICS and the infrastructure of content filtering, now that it exists we must be vigilant against potential abuses. We should make critical distinctions between the narrow but legitimate goals of content regulation—like providing mechanisms for parents to exercise control over what their children see—and the illegitimate uses to which these technologies can easily be applied.

> *"What we need is a wholesale reevaluation of our collective attitudes toward the meaning and value of free speech and the role it plays in our society."*

154

There are many ways in which we can subtly adjust the law of intellectual property, civil liability, and criminal law to tip the balance between more or less restrictive regimes of free speech, privacy, and individual expression. The federal government might limit the ability to claim intellectual property rights in lists of blocked sites. Such a policy would limit the profitability of commercial ventures that compiled them. We can also limit, as much as possible, Internet service providers' liability for what material flows through their hardware. This would remove one of the incentives that they would have for filtering content before it reached the individual user. Yet another tack is to rethink the civil liabilities we impose on employers when rogue employees download obscene or conceivably harassing material on their computer terminals. This, again, would remove at least one of the rationales for pervasive content filtering in the workplace. Sensible public policy can be devised to safeguard the values of an open society in the information age. But too often we are letting technology lead public policy around by the nose.

What we need is a wholesale reevaluation of our collective attitudes toward the meaning and value of free speech and the role it plays in our society. Though we strain mightily to avoid government censorship, there is little public commitment in our society today to a culture of free expression on its own merits. Public calls from Bill Bennett to shame media companies into "doing the right thing" are widely acclaimed. Political leaders too often take a wink-and-a-nod approach when private bodies take on the censoring role that government itself cannot. But the myopic focus on government as the singular or most significant threat to free speech rests on a basic misreading of our history. In America, the really pointed threats to free speech and free expression do not come from government. They never have. They have always come from willful majorities intent on bullying dissenters into silence. The new information technology and content filtering make that even more feasible than it has been in the past. And that is the problem.

# Chapter 4

# Should Government Funding of the Arts Be Restricted?

# Chapter Preface

The National Endowment for the Arts (NEA) is a federal program established in 1965 to promote the arts in America. With a current annual budget of $98 million, the agency makes grants to artists, as well as to museums and other institutions, in order to "foster the excellence, diversity and vitality of the arts in the United States and to broaden public access to the arts."

In recent years the NEA has been the target of a great deal of criticism. Critics of the agency generally protest the use of taxpayer funding to subsidize works they consider indecent, offensive, or just plain bad. They cite the example of performance artist Karen Finley, who was awarded NEA grants to smear her naked body with chocolate (which represents excrement) to illustrate the mistreatment of women. Citing this and other examples, many critics contend that the NEA should be abolished completely. Others advocate restrictions that would prevent the agency from supporting artists whose work is indecent, offensive, or obscene. NEA opponents are quick to reject the idea that artists' right to free speech includes the right to receive government funding for their efforts. As Edwin Feulner, president of the Heritage Foundation, states, "Artists have a legitimate First Amendment right to be as creative, or warped, as they want to be. But 'free speech' does not mean the taxpayer has to subsidize it."

Defenders of the NEA argue that government funding of the arts plays a crucial role in sustaining culture in America. They point out that such funding only costs taxpayers 36 cents a year and that an extremely small number of projects approved by the NEA are controversial. In addition, NEA supporters argue that placing restrictions on the content of art funded by the NEA violates artists' right to free expression. As the American Civil Liberties Union states, "When government seeks to legislate politically correct or 'respectful' art, it has violated the First Amendment, just as it would if it sought to legislate political correctness in a public university."

The debate over federal funding of the arts is the topic of the following chapter.

# Government Funding of the Arts Should End

## by David Boaz

**About the author:** *David Boaz is the executive vice president of the Cato Institute, a libertarian think tank.*

*Editor's note: The following viewpoint was prepared for delivery at the Delaware Center for Contemporary Arts on May 3, 1995.*

Art historian Alice Goldfarb Marquis wrote in the *New York Times*, "Twice in one recent week, my concert program contained a flyer headlined 'Warning! The performances you enjoy could be canceled!' This referred, of course, to the National Endowment for the Arts, presented as a pure virgin cruelly lashed to the railroad tracks."

The good news for the NEA, I suppose, is that on most of my recent train rides I've been presented with flyers reading, "Warning! This train could be canceled!" So maybe the Republican Congress will leave no trains to run over threatened virgins.

### The Individual vs. the State

Discussions of policy issues should begin with first principles. As my colleague Ed Crane notes, there are only two basic ways to organize society: coercively, through government dictates, or voluntarily, through the myriad interactions among individuals and private associations. All the various political "isms"—fascism, communism, conservatism, liberalism, neoconservatism— boil down to a single question. The bottom line of political philosophy, and therefore of politics itself, is, "Who is going to make the decision about this particular aspect of your life, you or somebody else?"

No matter what the philosophical debate, keep your eye on the bottom line: Politics is about the individual's relationship to the state, pure and simple.

Do you spend the money you earn or does some politician?

Reprinted from David Boaz, "The Separation of Art and State," speech delivered at the Delaware Center for Contemporary Arts, Wilmington, Delaware, May 3, 1995, by permission of the author.

Do you pick the school your child goes to or does some bureaucrat?

Do you decide what books you will read, or will some politician make that decision?

Do you decide what drugs to take when you're sick, or does a bureaucrat in Washington?

In a civil society you make the choices about your life. In a political society someone else makes those choices. And because it is not the natural order of things for someone other than you to make those decisions about your life, the political society is of necessity based on coercion.

> *"Congress has ignored the Constitution and assumed that it had the power to ban, require, regulate, or spend money on, anything under the sun."*

The American Founders understood this. That's why they declared, "All men are endowed by their creator with certain unalienable rights, that among these are life, liberty, and the pursuit of happiness," and why they wrote a Constitution that granted the federal government only a few enumerated and limited powers.

In 1794 James Madison, the father of the Constitution, rose on the floor of the House and declared that he could not "undertake to lay his finger on that article of the Federal Constitution which granted a right to Congress of expending, on objects of benevolence, the money of their constituents." Things had changed by 1935, when President Franklin Roosevelt wrote to Congress, "I hope your committee will not permit doubts as to constitutionality, however reasonable, to block the suggested legislation."

## Open Season on Taxpayers

Since then it's been open season on taxpayers' wallets. Congress has ignored the Constitution and assumed that it had the power to ban, require, regulate, or spend money on, anything under the sun.

And that's how we ended up here, discussing threats to artistic freedom from the 104th Congress. There would have been little fear of such threats from, say, the 54th Congress a century ago. The First Amendment prevented Congress from abridging freedom of speech, and the doctrine of enumerated powers meant that Congress couldn't involve itself in the arts at all. Emily Dickinson and Winslow Homer, Sinclair Lewis and Aaron Copland plied their trade blithely unaware of Congress.

Today, however, the federal Leviathan concerns itself with every nook and cranny of our lives, and the arts have not escaped its tender, stifling embrace.

## The Power of Art

I don't have to tell this audience about the importance of the arts, whether we're talking about literature, drama, painting, music, sculpture, or, lest I forget, dance. President John Kennedy—or one of his talented speechwriters—put it this way:

> Art establishes the basic human truths which must serve as the touchstones of our judgment. The artist, however faithful to his personal vision of reality, becomes the last champion of the individual mind and sensibility against an intrusive society and an officious state.

More recently, the managing director of Center Stage in Baltimore told the *Baltimore Sun*, "Art has power. It has the power to sustain, to heal, to humanize . . . to change something in you. It's a frightening power, and also a beautiful power. . . . And it's essential to a civilized society."

## Art Must Be Separate from Government

It is precisely because art has power, because it deals with basic human truths, that it must be kept separate from government. Government, as I noted earlier, involves the organization of coercion. In a free society coercion should be reserved only for such essential functions of government as protecting rights and punishing criminals. People should not be forced to contribute money to artistic endeavors that they may not approve, nor should artists be forced to trim their sails to meet government standards.

Government funding of anything involves government control. That insight, of course, is part of our folk wisdom: "He who pays the piper calls the tune." "Who takes the king's shilling sings the king's song."

> *"People should not be forced to contribute money to artistic endeavors that they may not approve."*

Defenders of arts funding seem blithely unaware of this danger when they praise the role of the national endowments as an imprimatur or seal of approval on artists and arts groups. Jane Alexander says, "The Federal role is small but very vital. We are a stimulus for leveraging state, local and private money. We are a linchpin for the puzzle of arts funding, a remarkably efficient way of stimulating private money." Drama critic Robert Brustein asks, "How could the NEA be 'privatized' and still retain its purpose as a funding agency functioning as a stamp of approval for deserving art?"

In 1981, as conservative factions battled for control of the National Endowment for the Humanities, Richard Goldstein of the *Village Voice* explained the consequences this way:

> The NEH has a ripple effect on university hiring and tenure, and on the kinds of research undertaken by scholars seeking support. Its chairman shapes the bounds of that support. In a broad sense, he sets standards that affect the tenor of textbooks and the content of curricula. . . . Though no chairman of the NEH can single-handedly direct the course of American education, he can nurture the nascent trends and take advantage of informal opportunities to signal department heads and deans. He can "persuade" with the cudgel of federal funding out of sight but hardly out of mind.

I suggest that that is just the kind of power no government in a free society should have.

It is often said that other governments have long subsidized the arts. True, but as Jonathan Yardley, book critic for the *Washington Post*, points out, the examples usually cited are of autocratic, even tyrannical governments. Do we really want our government to emulate the Roman Empire, or the Medicis, or Louis XIV?

Now it's also true that the social democracies of Western Europe sub-

> *"Do we really want our government to emulate the Roman Empire, or the Medicis, or Louis XIV?"*

sidize the arts more extensively than we do. But those countries too are different in important ways from the United States. First, as Yardley says, "they are accustomed to state influences (in religion as in the arts) that our ancestors crossed the ocean to escape." As we should not want an established church, so we should not want established art. Second, the European countries are small and homogeneous compared with the United States. Thus they can "reach consensus on certain matters that we, precisely because we cannot agree on them, prefer to keep out of the hands of government." No European country was founded on the principles of the Declaration of Independence, nor does any European country have such a limited government.

Let me take just a moment to note that the amount of arts funding in the federal budget is quite small. That might be taken as a defense of the funding, were it not for the important reasons to avoid any government funding of something as intimate yet powerful as artistic expression. I bring up the dollar amount for another reason—to point out how small it is as a percentage of the total arts budget in this country. The National Endowment for the Arts has a budget of $167 million—less than 2 percent of the over $9 billion in private contributions to the arts from corporations, foundations, and individuals in 1993. According to the chair of the American Arts Alliance, the arts are a $37 billion industry. Surely they will survive without whatever portion of the NEA's budget gets out of the Washington bureaucracy and into the hands of actual artists or arts institutions. [Editor's note: The NEA's budget was reduced to less than $100 million a year beginning in 1996.]

## The Taxpayer's Perspective

So far I've looked at arts funding from the perspective of art and political philosophy. Let me take just a moment to consider the taxpayer's perspective. In that marvelous British television show, "Yes, Minister," Sir Humphrey Appleby once said, "Subsidy is for art, for culture. It is not to be given to what the people want. It is for what the people don't want but ought to have. If they want something, they'll pay for it themselves."

Take a typical American taxpayer. She's on her feet eight hours a day selling blue jeans at Wal-Mart. She serves spaghetti twice a week because meat is expensive, and when she can scrape together a little extra she likes to hear Randy Travis or take her daughter to see Mariah Carey. Now what gives us the right to tax her so that lawyers and lobbyists can save a few bucks on Kennedy Center tickets?

Thus the case against government funding of the arts. But the question posed tonight is not, "Should the government fund the arts?" but "How will the 104th Congress affect artistic freedom?" If Congress takes my advice and eliminates the endowments, artistic freedom will be better protected than ever before. But alas, Congress frequently ignores my advice, and as long as government funding remains, there is a real threat of government meddling in the arts.

## The Separation of Art and State

The latest newsletter from People for the American Way identifies a lot of threats to free expression. Some involve an actual assault on private actions—such as censorship of the Internet, a ban on flag-burning, a denial of tax exemption to groups that support ideas some congressman doesn't like—and fortunately the First Amendment will protect us from most of these. But most of them involve restrictions on the way government funds can be used. Duke University law professor Walter Dellinger, now a member of the Clinton White House, warned recently that such rules are "especially alarming in light of the growing role of government as subsidizer, landlord, employer and patron of the arts."

Dellinger is right. But the only way to solve the problem he raises is to reduce the government's role in society. Surely we can't expect taxpayers just to hand over $1.5 trillion a year to various agencies and interests without regulating how the money is spent. Their representatives in Congress and the administration think that those who are paying for the education, or the art, or the medical care have a right to say just what they will and will not pay for.

Thus the Georgia legislature punishes Georgia Public Television for the PBS broadcast of *Tales of the City*. Thus Congress bars the arts endowment from funding obscene work. Thus public schools are pressured not to teach *Huckleberry Finn*. Thus the director of the National Air and Space Museum is forced to resign after criticism of an exhibit on the bombing of Japan. Whether the pressure comes

> *"As long as government funding remains, there is a real threat of government meddling in the arts."*

from Jesse Helms or Jesse Jackson, the Rainbow Coalition or the Christian Coalition, taxpayers' money is subject to political control. On NPR [National Public Radio] this morning, an activist complained about the forced resignation of the museum director, saying, "My ancestors didn't fight for the concept of official history in official museums." But when you have official museums, or a National Endowment for the Arts serving as a "seal of approval" for artists, you

162

get official history and official art—and citizens will fight over just which history and which art should have that imprimatur.

We fought these battles before, in the Wars of Religion.

The American Founders knew that the solution was the separation of church and state. Because art is just as spiritual, just as meaningful, just as powerful as religion, it is time to grant art the same independence and respect that religion has. It is time to establish the separation of art and state.

# Government Should Not Fund Obscene Art

**by John Leo**

**About the author:** *John Leo is a syndicated columnist and a contributing editor for* U.S. News & World Report.

Call me perverse, but I spent an evening last week checking out Karen Finley's new act. Trivia buffs will recall Finley as the chocolate-covered nude performer who did colorful things with yams and federal arts money in 1990, thus attracting great attention as either an embattled artist or a national laughingstock, depending on your point of view.

Return of the Chocolate-Smeared Woman was staged in a tiny theater in lower Manhattan, with the audience sitting quietly in amazing discomfort on empty paint buckets instead of chairs. The warm-up act, the Dancing Furballs, consisted of several chocolate-marked young people dancing with enthusiasm but not much coordination. Other Furballs distributed free glasses of beer and wine, perhaps to compensate for the theater's version of bucket seating.

Finley then appeared and immediately took off her dress. Wearing only panties and gold high-heeled shoes, she began smearing her body with chocolate and asked if anybody in the audience would like to come up and take a lick for $20.

## A Dated Tirade

This is an odd way to begin a show, particularly since the chocolate is supposed to represent excrement and what men like to do to women's bodies. But art is art, and two women in the audience finally were coaxed onstage to lick a bit of chocolate off one thigh and one belly button. The licking apparently concluded the lighthearted section of the program, because Finley quickly launched into her familiar tirade mode.

The *Washington Post* once described Finley as "an impassioned voice in the wilderness, crying out against perceived injustice." Another way of putting this is to say that she thinks heterosexual males are pigs, and she is always eager to share this insight at the top of her lungs. Sure enough, we begin to hear about fathers, preachers, and doctors who molest and rape children, and policemen who show up eagerly at rape scenes to demand oral sex from the victims. This dark worldview is right out of the radical males-are-evil feminism of Catharine MacKinnon and Andrea Dworkin. But at least MacKinnon and Dworkin know how to write. Finley's tirade is an angry jumble that comes nowhere near the emotional effect she apparently intends to have.

Wanted: new material. Every time Finley uses the word "love," it is immediately connected to some form of abuse or hatred. The message seems to be that men are incapable of affection and loyalty. The tentacles of the evil patriarchy are everywhere. To enjoy this show, it is clearly best to have the opinion that women are helpless victims of brutish men. The audience seems to be filled with attractive and successful-looking women who have paid $20 to hear Finley's essentially hopeless message of female victimization.

Among other things, Finley's diatribe seems badly dated. If new material has been added since her first chocolate-smeared headlines, it's not really apparent. Complaining about male perfidy may have been the frontier in 1990, but women have moved on and upward. Nobody seems to have told Finley. This may be why the audience doesn't seem thrilled by this act.

Only once does Finley seem to be working material with some power: when she speaks of the loss of friends who died of AIDS. But this is a rerun of her 1990 performance, and she neatly undercuts it by delivering the monologue while sitting completely naked in a washtub, scrubbing off the chocolate and assorted sticky things. We are supposed to believe that the scrubbing is symbolically significant (Finley tells us two or three times that it represents "starting over"), but it's hard to believe that the audience is fully engaged in the horror of AIDS while Finley is working so hard on her personal chocolate removal.

## Lame Ramble

Finley launches into a gross monologue about having sex with Kenneth Starr, Jesse Helms, Orrin Hatch, Ted Kennedy, and Bill Clinton. She is the star, lusted after by weird and terrible men. Message: Look at me—I'm saying provocative sexual things about well-known politicians! An unusually pointless monologue depicts Bill having sex with Hillary. Yes, it's surely indecent, but the main problem is that her ramble is so lame, scrubbed clean of any humor, cleverness, or insight. How can she miss targets this huge? Her material "is more inflammatory than insightful," the *Washington Post* said delicately, adding that Finley "goads one into heavy ponderings."

> *"Finley's tirade is an angry jumble that comes nowhere near the emotional effect she apparently intends to have."*

The last phrase is true. I myself was goaded into an unusually heavy pondering on why anyone who is not a columnist would want to sit through this stuff. If she is an artist, so is the drunk on the next bar stool whimpering about how awful women are. I also experienced a backup ponder. It focused on why the taxpayers would want to invest in this with public funds that could more defensibly be spent on those $600 Pentagon-designed toilet seats.

*"Everything counts as art these days."*

The answer, I suppose, is obvious. Everything counts as art these days. This is particularly true of art-free politicized rants from the cultural left, which helpfully supplied most of the judges who awarded the dubious performance-art grants before political pressure cut them off. The Supreme Court now says, in effect, that we don't have to genuflect to this system by continuing to fund craziness described as art. Be grateful.

# The Arts Will Thrive Without the National Endowment for the Arts

by William Craig Rice

**About the author:** *William Craig Rice is a preceptor in expository writing at Harvard University and a fellow at the Heritage Foundation, a conservative think tank.*

The death knell is sounding for the National Endowment for the Arts. The agency's federal appropriation in 1996 fell by one-third, from about $150 million to about $100 million, and its appropriation may be cut again or even eliminated. The NEA is not only anathema to cultural conservatives, libertarians, evangelical Christians, and even a good number of artists. It is also likely to lose key political support as President Bill Clinton and other Democrats resolve to keep moving toward a balanced federal budget without compromising Medicare, Medicaid, education, or the environment.

But the end of the agency's federal funding need not prove cataclysmic for the arts in America. Artists, arts organizations, and their supporters have many strategies at their disposal for maintaining the vitality of the arts in a post-NEA era. And in any case, the importance of federal grantmaking to the arts has been greatly exaggerated.

## Two Forms of Support

The NEA currently contributes to the arts in two ways: direct funding and less tangible, indirect services. Nowadays direct funding consists almost entirely of cash awards to arts organizations and event sponsors. (As of 1996, grants to individual artists were eliminated, except for creative writers, jazz greats, and masters of folk crafts.) NEA-financed music ensembles, dance festivals, museum exhibitions, and the like undoubtedly face a period of sacrifice and uncertainty, and there will be some casualties. But their prospects are far from hopeless.

Excerpted from William Craig Rice, "I Hear America Singing: The Arts Will Flower Without the NEA," *Policy Review*, March/April 1997. Reprinted with permission of *Policy Review*, a publication of The Heritage Foundation.

The NEA also renders indirect, noncash benefits and services through its peer-review panels. Their judgments can stimulate funding from other sources and identify certain artists and organizations as more deserving than others. In this realm of power-by-imprimatur, the judgment process would, in fact, probably work better if it were decentralized and used to spur greater involvement by funders.

## Favoring Elite Establishments

To understand the reasons for optimism, it is necessary to assess the true nature of NEA spending priorities. The NEA's largesse regularly benefits the great established urban institutions and smaller local organizations of long-standing reputation. The NEA has also funded, less dependably, dozens of marginal artistic groups, some of which claim to depend on NEA funding for their survival. As a rule, the larger institutions will overcome the NEA's decline easily, but the smaller ones need not suffer if they heed certain examples set around the country.

One might not know it from the political controversies that have attracted public attention, but the NEA has always favored the most venerable—and richest—cultural establishments over the esoteric, the shocking, and the avant-garde. A survey of funding patterns in 1985, 1990, and 1995 clearly reveals this preference. The Metropolitan Opera in New York City has been the single largest recipient of NEA funds, with annual grants between $800,000 and $900,000. Typical grants for other high-profile beneficiaries range from $200,000 to $350,000, awarded year after year and now incorporated into annual budgets. In theater, by far the biggest ongoing grants go to the major presenters and training centers, such as the American Repertory Theater in Cambridge, Massachusetts ($305,000, on average, in 1985, 1990, and 1995), the Center Theater Group of Los Angeles ($251,000), the Guthrie Theater in Minneapolis ($274,000), and the Yale Repertory Theatre ($167,000).

In the museum world, the consistent winners are big-city institutions: Boston, Chicago, Detroit, Los Angeles, New York, Philadelphia, San Francisco. In dance as well, the NEA has heavily favored the most established organizations. The Dance Theatre of Harlem, for example, averaged $303,000. Nearly all other troupes with six-figure grants bear the names of modern American legends: Alvin Ailey, Merce Cunningham, Martha Graham, Paul Taylor, Twyla Tharp.

> *"The end of the [NEA's] federal funding need not prove cataclysmic for the arts in America."*

This preference for elite establishments should not be surprising, since it is usually the larger, wealthier institutions that have the staff and resources to put together winning grant proposals. The higher the grant amount, the more this pattern holds true. The NEA's differential treatment of arts institutions confirms economist Friedrich Hayek's dictum that centralized authority inevitably favors the rich and well-educated because they have greater access to the sites and protocols of power. NEA support for music in the state of Pennsylvania at the height of the NEA's prowess in 1985 emphatically illustrates this. Grants that year overwhelmingly favored the Philadelphia Orchestra and Pittsburgh Symphony, which received $290,000 and $280,000, respectively. All the remaining grants that year—to 28 Pennsylvania musical organizations—totaled $301,000.

## Tiddlywinks

At first blush, six-figure grants to our most revered institutions may appear difficult to replace, and the potential damage from cuts quite dire. But on examination it is hard not to reach the opposite conclusion. The NEA's largest grants are tiddlywinks to the big players in American culture.

*Music.* Take the leading example, the Metropolitan Opera. Using conservative estimates, its annual $875,000 dependency could be made up by raising the price of tickets, which already cost $125 and up, by $1.50. For the Philadelphia Orchestra, Pittsburgh Symphony, and other great American orchestras, a hike in ticket prices of less than $2 would replace any shortfall in NEA funds. The Boston Symphony Orchestra received only $300,000 of its $47 million operating budget from the NEA in 1996—less than 1 percent of the total, or 40 cents per ticket sold that year for BSO, Boston Pops, and Tanglewood Festival concerts.

> *"For the Philadelphia Orchestra, . . . a hike in ticket prices of less than $2 would replace any shortfall in NEA funds."*

*Museums.* The Art Institute of Chicago has received about $325,000 a year from the NEA, but this is only 1 percent of its budget. The Walker Art Center of Minneapolis received 3.3 percent of its budget in 1995 from the NEA, down from 8.2 percent in 1985. The importance of federal support has declined as individual gifts, foundation grants, and investment income have risen.

*Dance.* Although modern dance began as an esoteric experiment, performances now enjoy broad popularity with American audiences. If raising ticket prices is a less feasible solution to looming financial shortfalls, modern dance should have a good chance of winning corporate support. According to a recent analysis reported in the *Chronicle of Philanthropy*, corporate giving to the arts, especially in the once-generous financial services sector, has drifted away from symphonies and arts associated with the wealthy; it now focuses on causes with more popular appeal. Modern dance, seeking corporate support in this new environment, can cite its origin in the United States and its roots in our cultural diversity as well as its popularity.

*Theater.* The major outlets for professional theater face huge challenges as well. Robert Brustein, one of the foremost trainers of new theater talent, writes in *Theater* magazine that "as funds dry up for the arts in this country, and theater grows increasingly estranged from younger audiences, there is no question that the marketplace will play a larger and larger role in the non-profit future." For Brustein and most other theater people, the marketplace is no talisman of artistic excellence, driven as it is by consumer taste and capitalism, which tend to impinge on artistic freedom and dilute quality in favor of popular appeal. But there are ways that commerce could be enlisted to sustain live theater.

Hollywood, for example, has been 20th-century America's great patron of actors, as well as of writers from William Faulkner and F. Scott Fitzgerald onward. That patronage must be expanded if fresh talent in acting, screenwriting, and production is to continue to flow into studios from the far-flung theater world. Theater and cultural critic Frank Rich of the *New York Times* urges "people who run movie studios, many of whom have talented executives who came out of the non-profit theater world or the non-profit film world, to put something back in [by] training non-profit theaters to market better."

> *"There are ways that commerce could be enlisted to sustain live theater."*

In fairness, some actors and producers have used their money to create opportunity in their field. One of the principal beneficiaries is the University of Southern California, which boasts the Steven Spielberg Scoring Studio and two buildings erected by producer and director George Lucas. Actor John Ritter endowed a Town and Gown Scholarship; Jack Nicholson an acting award. James and Nony Doolittle, L.A.'s leading theatrical producers, created a fund to assist recent USC graduates making the transition to professional acting.

But considering the huge fortunes involved, Hollywood moguls and stars could do much more to assure the long-term health of the professional stage—and amateur stage, for that matter—perhaps through such existing professional societies and philanthropies as Actors Equity, the Shubert Foundation (which Brustein praises), and the National Corporate Theater Fund. . . .

## Philanthropy for Writers

Ideally, the decline of the NEA will usher in an era of imaginative philanthropy. In this regard, we can glean mixed lessons from the support that has historically been available to creative writers. Every year since 1985, 10 or so young authors—novelists, poets, and essayists with one or two books to their credit—receive a phone call out of the blue from the Mrs. Giles Whiting Foundation. The Whiting Writers' Awards, currently $30,000 each, are enough to stake frugal writers to at least one highly productive year on whatever projects they wish, no strings attached. (The NEA awards to writers are lower—$20,000 apiece—and require an elaborate application process that favors those skilled in bureaucratic ways.)

A second model of support for needy writers once came from the initiative of the late poet James Merrill. With income from his Merrill Lynch inheritance, he established the Ingram-Merrill Foundation with an active, voting board. From the late 1950s until his death in 1995, when the foundation spent itself out of existence, struggling writers could apply for small or large cash grants. Merrill set an admirable and imaginative example of generosity that other artists of means can well follow, especially if they want a shield between their friendships and their philanthropy, as Merrill did.

Long before the growth of Master of Fine Arts (MFA) programs, the cause of creative writing was furthered by a few thoughtfully envisioned philanthropies for writers in universities. The American playwright Avery T. Hopwood bequeathed a sizable trust for creative writing awards at the University of Michigan in the 1920s, when Robert Frost was writer-in-residence. According to Nicholas Delbanco in *Speaking of Writing: Selected Hopwood Lectures*, more than $1 million in prizes went to student writers in the award's first 60 years; about $45,000 is now given annually. Beyond encouraging young writers, the legacy has attracted more endowed awards, helping to create a literary environment that supported W.H. Auden, Robert Hayden, Theodore Roethke, and others since. The Wallace Stegner Fellowships at Stanford University, endowed by the Jones family in 1945, have also long sustained emerging writers, including Scott Turow, who recently endowed a writing fellowship in honor of his Stanford teacher Richard Scowcroft. . . .

## What of the Future?

It is impossible to predict with confidence what will happen to arts philanthropy in a post-NEA world. Critics of government programs in general claim that public spending tends to discourage private support. Critics of the NEA in particular contend that it stepped in to fund arts programs previously supported by the Ford and Rockefeller Foundations. And as Alice Goldfarb Marquis shows in her excellent history, *Art Lessons: Learning from the Decline and Fall of Public Arts Funding*, federal involvement in the arts in the 1960s did spring from the initiative of a few influential foundations and studies by affiliated scholars.

Federal support may well have allowed Ford and Rockefeller to move on to other ventures, but the last 30 years have hardly lacked for gifts to the arts, the multibillion-dollar Getty Trust foremost among them. (Its annual expenditures run well ahead of the NEA budget.) H. Ross Perot donated the Morton H. Meyerson Symphony Center, an acoustic wonder that houses the Dallas Symphony, in honor of his friend and business associate. Successful artists have pitched in (listen up, Hollywood) to establish the Krasner-Pollock, Warhol, Gottlieb, and Mapplethorpe foundations. In St. Louis, E. Desmond Lee

> *"Ideally, the decline of the NEA will usher in an era of imaginative philanthropy."*

paid off his city symphony's multimillion-dollar debt to the state of Missouri. In Hastings-on-Hudson, New York, Barbara E. Newington recently established the Newington-Cropsey Foundation on the site of her great-grandfather Jasper Francis Cropsey's restored art studio. The foundation exhibits Hudson River School and new figurative painters, operates an atelier for apprentice sculptors, and publishes *American Arts Quarterly*, a journal devoted to movements in architecture, sculpture, and painting that challenge the orthodoxies of late modernism and postmodernism.

Dozens of other examples could be listed, but imaginative supporters of the arts will need to look beyond philanthropy. The arts must embrace their own commercial potential and disregard the embarrassment of lingering elites. Museums now realize a good portion of their income from gift shops and restaurants and from facilities rentals. Orchestras get a healthy take from sales of their recordings. Critics rightly snipe at the "malling" of museums, where posters, gewgaws, and nouvelle cuisine distract attention from the paintings, and at the commercialization of classical music, which plasters comely young soloists on CD covers. But the more art lovers—and artists—that emerge, the more likely it is that fresh commercial approaches will appear. All this will be in keeping with the American way of art. New experiments by young New York artists, who are using makeshift spaces and temporary storefronts to show their work, may herald a shift toward a less intimidating art marketplace.

> *"The arts must embrace their own commercial potential."*

## The NEA's Leverage

It is often argued in defense of the NEA that private and nonprofit supporters of the arts have come to rely on the authority of an NEA grant in making their own award decisions. The process works like this: The NEA's panels of experts in, say, dance or creative writing or sculpture give the nod to a certain troupe, small press, or exhibit. Then a private foundation or local agency decides it may safely favor an application from the same group—and spare itself the expense of evaluating the proposal. Some arts administrators say they spend more resources applying for an NEA grant than the grant itself is worth, simply because they need the grant as "leverage" with other funding sources. NEA Chairwoman Jane Alexander claims that NEA grants generate other support at a rate of 12 to 1, making a $10,000 NEA grant worth $120,000. More conservative estimates run as high as 7 to 1 and as low as 3 to 1—still significant leverage.

The NEA's leverage can be seen as a welcome asset bestowed upon arts organizations, but it can just as easily be read as a device for self-aggrandizement. The process gives the NEA a vastly disproportionate role in deciding what and who gets the advantage, and it has a strong centralizing and professionalizing effect. According to some observers, this undermines the health of the arts themselves by divorcing them from local, nonexpert constituencies, people who enjoy the arts but have no professional stake in them. NEA critic Laurence Jarvik recently argued in *Common Sense* in favor of decentralized mechanisms of judgment. "Patrons," he notes, "would have to take fuller responsibility for their own decisions—and local arts groups would have the freedom to consider the tastes of the local communities they serve without regard to the opinions of a federal agency."

> *"Several options suggest themselves for replacing the judging services rendered by the NEA."*

Without debating too deeply the wisdom of concentrating cultural power in government-appointed bodies, the question arises: How can the work of expert advisory panels be replaced or otherwise performed?

The answer is surprisingly simple. The panels have doubtless saved money for foundations and other arts supporters large and small, who will soon have to retain their own judges to evaluate the applications they receive. Yet the portion of the NEA budget set aside for professional panels is minuscule. In 1995, the NEA spent $924,000 on panelists' honoraria and travel expenses; in 1996, after budget cuts, $476,000. These figures account for only about 0.5 percent of the annual NEA budget.

## Other Options

Several options suggest themselves for replacing the judging services rendered by the NEA, some resembling the old system, others quite different. Centralized arts organizations already exist in all the fields adjudicated by NEA panelists; many of them already have panels that make awards to individuals and organizations. In the field of writing, these include the PEN American Center, the Academy of American Poets, the Poetry Society of America, and Associated Writing Programs. In music, they include Opera America, the Center for Contemporary Opera, the American Symphony Orchestra League, and the International Conference of Symphony and Opera Musicians. Composers have the National Association of Composers and the Composer's Theatre. Drama is well-endowed with prizes and professionally well-organized under the National Critics Institute, National Corporate Theater Fund, and the New York Drama Critics Circle, which confers important awards.

All these organizations and at least a dozen more can—or already do—impanel experts from their own ranks, as can the larger museums and universities. Further, the Getty Trust, the MacArthur Fellows Program, the Guggenheim, and other prominent philanthropies currently appoint their own judges. In metropolitan areas where artists and arts professionals are abundant, local talent could offer to certify the value of artistic work under consideration for funding, thereby cutting travel expenses. By and large, panels of this sort would resemble the old NEA methodology of centralized expertise and elite professionalism.

But this isn't the only model. Interesting arrangements could arise from a pro-liferation of judging mechanisms. Let a thousand flowers—or judges—bloom, from small self-selected groups to regional consortia, from impresarios to ad hoc committees, from local patrons to democratically elected bodies, each vari-ously set up to review public art commissions, individual grant proposals, theater-aid packages, endowment campaigns, and the like. These alternative models would take advantage of Americans' penchant for voluntary associa-tions and reverse the controversial rise of elite expert culture in the arts. If judg-ing systems were opened up, if interested lay persons enjoyed more than token status in the evaluation process, it is conceivable that support for the arts would actually broaden.

## A Lesson from History

Finally, we need to remember how little American art has ever originated from government grants. Except for sculpture, where 19th-century heroic statu-ary by the likes of Augustus Saint Gaudens and Anne Whitney came from pub-lic commissions, virtually all our best music, literature, painting, dance, and theater sprang from unexpected or unpromising corners. This happened, as the historian Neil Harris notes, in a new nation that lacked traditional European sources of patronage: a state church, a monarch, an aristocracy. For a long time, artists were itinerant figures, painting portraits and homesteads, staging plays and operas, giving recitals and readings, accumulating a tradition of hardship and irreverent individualism that persists in cultural memory—and reality—to this day.

Important painters as often as not drew their inspiration from and worked out-side the urban centers, from the Rocky Mountain and Hudson River painters in the 19th century to masters in the 20th: Grant Wood and Thomas Hart Benton in the Midwest, O'Keeffe in the Southwest desert, Winslow Homer in coastal Maine, Andrew Wyeth in Pennsylvania. Regionalism not only defines a large portion of American art history; it also helps account for the exciting resur-gence of landscape and realist painting today, itself partly a reaction to the tire-some domination of abstraction and conceptualism in major art centers and schools. In this historical con-text, the demise of the NEA as a powerful centralized authority may augur well for American painting.

> *"We need to remember how little American art has ever originated from government grants."*

Much—perhaps most—of our best work in literature and music in this century has come from outside the centers of money and prestige. The South, our least literate region, gave us great writ-ers like William Faulkner, Flannery O'Connor, Zora Neale Hurston, and John Kennedy Toole. African Americans broke through poverty and race barriers to create the world's most influential music in this century: Louis Armstrong,

Duke Ellington, Bessie Smith, Charlie Parker, Ella Fitzgerald, Leadbelly, Muddy Waters, Miles Davis, John Coltrane, Jimi Hendrix.

If most of the artists I have cited here—and there are dozens more—hailed from unexpected places and stations and faced real struggles, most also got along pretty well or actually prospered. Far from suffering from the Van Gogh syndrome—that tragic complex of poverty, neglect, mad genius, and sexual dysfunction—artists in American history present us with conflicting examples of stalwart individualism and courtly charm, business acumen and hopeless profligacy, indifference to the judgment of established critics and eager pursuit of honors from professional societies. In the twilight of the National Endowment for the Arts, it is the stalwarts, the pertinacious, entrepreneurial, independent spirits—and those with the vision to help them—who stand the chance of advancing the cause of American Art.

*"The demise of the NEA as a powerful centralized authority may augur well for American painting."*

# Federal Funding of the Arts Should Not End

by American Arts Alliance

**About the author:** *American Arts Alliance is a lobbying organization that advocates for government funding of nonprofit arts organizations.*

MYTH: *The federal government should not support the arts and culture.*

FACT: Americans value the arts and culture in their lives. All great nations support the arts. Recognizing that the not-for-profit arts are vital to a society's well-being and that they could not survive without public patronage, national governments throughout history have helped nurture and sustain cultural activity. Future generations will judge this era of our country's life by the level of our national commitment to supporting the finest expressions of the human condition. The United States today spends 36 cents per capita to support the National Endowment for the Arts. National support also helps Americans share their diverse cultures with one another. Grants from the National Arts Endowment (NEA) encourage performing arts groups to travel outside their states, often to rural areas which are traditionally underserved by the arts, and also help regionally based cultures reach wider audiences outside their indigenous areas. In creating the NEA in 1965, the Congress wisely noted that "An advanced civilization must not limit its efforts to science and technology alone, but must give full value and support to the other great branches of scholarly and cultural activity in order to achieve a better understanding of the past, a better analysis of the present, and a better view of the future."

## The Benefits of Arts Funding

MYTH: *The federal government cannot afford to fund arts and cultural programs at a time of fiscal restraint. Furthermore, the arts are a frill.*

FACT: Cultural funding is less than one one-hundredth of one percent (.001%) of the federal government's multi-billion dollar budget, and a mere 36 cents per capita. If the NEA is to be cut for budget reasons, that is on economic grounds, then the agency should be analyzed in economic terms. Doing so re-

Reprinted, with permission, from the American Arts Alliance online publication "Dispelling Myths About National Support of the Arts and Culture," June 26, 1998, at www.artswire.org/~aaa/myth.html. For the latest version of this publication, visit the website.

veals that cutting funding would not help decrease the deficit. In fact, data suggests such a cut could increase the deficit and actually would hurt local economies. The arts attract tourist dollars, stimulate business development, spur urban renewal, attract new businesses, and improve the overall quality of life for our cities and towns. On a national level, the not-for-profit arts create $37 billion in economic activity and support 1.3 million jobs. They also return $3.4 billion to the federal treasury through income taxes. Each year, the Arts Endowment opens the door to the arts to millions of schoolchildren, including "at-risk" youth. The arts are essential for our children's future because they improve overall student learning, enhance cognitive development, instill self-esteem and discipline, and provide creative outlets for self-expression. The arts also help prepare America's future high-tech work force by helping students develop problem-solving and reasoning skills, hone communication ability, and expand creativity—all important career skills in the 21st century labor market. Furthermore, artists, arts institutions and organizations make a positive economic impact on their surrounding communities, strengthening the local economy.

> *"Cultural funding is less than one one-hundredth of one percent (.001%) of the federal government's multi-billion dollar budget."*

MYTH: *The NEA is "elitist," a subsidy for the upper-class.*

FACT: The NEA increases access to arts and culture, thereby improving a community's quality of life for all its citizens. The NEA also helps support community festivals, rural chamber music, arts centers, galleries and the arts in libraries, town halls, children's organizations, and other social and civic institutions where families can experience the arts. In fact, without public support, the not-for-profit arts would become the sole province of the well-to-do.

MYTH: *Americans don't want the federal government to continue supporting the arts and culture.*

FACT: On the contrary, a majority of Americans support federal funding for the arts and culture. A recent Lou Harris poll indicated that 79 percent of Americans believe that "the federal government should provide financial assistance to arts organizations, such as arts museums, dance, opera, theater groups, and symphony orchestras." Almost as many, 61 percent, say they "would be willing to pay $5 more in their own taxes per year to support federal government efforts in the arts."

## Private Giving and the Marketplace

MYTH: *The loss of public funding for the arts will readily be replaced by the private sector.*

FACT: The presumption that private giving will supplant any loss of federal funds is without foundation. In fact, corporate support for the arts has been declining over the past decade. Although many of the highest quality arts organizations are filling their houses for virtually every performance, they are operating at deficits of over $1 million. Despite the fact that ticket sales and other earned income are higher than ever before, escalating costs have made it increasingly difficult for not-for-profit arts groups to make ends meet. Average to large size symphony orchestras, for example, must raise an average of $42 per seat per performance over and above ticket prices just to break even. Arts organizations work tirelessly at fundraising, exploring every possibility to cultivate new sources of revenue. Grants from the Arts Endowment not only provide vital funds in and of themselves, but the leveraging effect of these grants, which require at least a dollar-for-dollar match, stimulates private giving many times over the required match. Taking away the federal "seed" money will not encourage arts funding to grow, but will result in just the opposite.

MYTH: *The best of the arts will survive in the open market.*

FACT: As stated in a recent newspaper article, "history shows few correlations between what is popular enough to pay for itself and what is good enough to last. . . . Great art is rarely created with popularity in mind." The not-for-profit arts have never been able to sustain themselves in the commercial market, nor does the marketplace necessarily reflect the most enduring expression of a civilized society.

MYTH: *The states are better suited to support the arts.*

FACT: Grants from the NEA are a matter of national prestige, a stamp of excellence that relies on an exten-

> *"Seventy-nine percent of Americans believe that 'the federal government should provide financial assistance to arts organizations.'"*

sive, democratic and highly regarded system of peer review. The agency's funding decisions provide valued direction to private and corporate funders. The Endowment is uniquely positioned to support projects that serve the whole nation and help Americans share their diverse cultures with one another. NEA funding encourages performing arts groups to travel outside their states, often to rural areas which are traditionally underserved by the arts.

## Speech and the Constitution

MYTH: *Because government does not subsidize speech, government should not support the arts.*

FACT: In fact, the government does support speech. A review of the federal budget reveals many areas in which government supports speech including: education programs, the Congressional Record, the Government Printing Office and Presidential candidates with campaign financing. Furthermore, government, through the American taxpayer, subsidizes the speech of our elected officials.

MYTH: *Arts funding is not in the Constitution.*

FACT: The Constitution has proven a valuable charter of government for more than two centuries because it is not a document of specifics. In fact, our Constitution is now one of the world's oldest because, as many scholars assert, it is the shortest and is rarely amended. Our Constitution is enduring because it generally does not articulate specifics. Many programs, such as Social Security, are not specified in the Constitution. However, this program and others are supported by the American people because the Constitution does give broad power to Congress to "promote" the general welfare, as stated in its preamble.

# Decency Restrictions on Arts Funding Threaten Free Speech

by Marcia Pally

About the author: *Marcia Pally is the author of numerous articles on censorship as well as the books* Sense and Censorship: The Vanity of Bonfires *and* Sex & Sensibility: Reflections on Forbidden Mirrors and the Will to Censor.

In the late 1980s, performance artist and NEA grant recipient Karen Finley took off her clothes and smeared herself with chocolate to symbolize the shit women put up with. Most of the audience at the 1 AM performance I saw thought Finley's feminist point was emphatic, if messy, but leaders of the political and religious right did not see it that way—at least as they read about it in the papers. They saw Finley's piece as an unnecessarily pornographic way of expressing oneself which decent people shouldn't have to pay taxes to support. They complained to Congress, and Finley and three other artists whose work addressed AIDS or (homo)sexuality—John Fleck, Holly Hughes, Tim Miller—lost their grants. In return, the artists sued the government, accusing the NEA of discriminating against them on the basis of their ideas, thereby violating Constitutional guarantees of freedom of expression. Thus was the beginning of the nine-year court fight that ended on June 25, 1998, when the Supreme Court, in "The National Endowment for the Arts (NEA) v. Karen Finley *et al.*," upheld the now-famous "decency test" for NEA grants. That decision has broad implications—though at the moment, unclear ones—not only for American art but for all public programs that fund the ideas, research, or expression of Americans.

## Attempts to Legislate Decency

In 1989, during the controversy that followed Ms. Finley's new clothes, Congress passed its first law prohibiting the NEA from funding provocative art. Reflecting the conservative shift in Congress during the Reagan and Bush admin-

Excerpted from Marcia Pally, "'Decency' in the Arts," *Tikkun*, November/December 1998. Reprinted by permission of *Tikkun: A Bimonthly Jewish Critique of Politics, Culture and Society.*

istrations, the law prohibited NEA grants for art that is obscene, sadomasochistic, homoerotic or that depicts the sexual exploitation of children. The statute was declared unconstitutional in 1991 (in a case called Bella Lewitzky Dance Foundation v. Frohnmeyer)—not only because the broad prohibition against homoeroticism and sadomasochism disqualified much of Western art (including images of the Crucifixion) but also because the Supreme Court reaffirmed that government may not discriminate against the ideas of its citizens.

> *"What precisely is 'decency'?*
> *... Whose 'standards,'*
> *'beliefs,' and 'values'*
> *should artists respect?"*

In 1990, when it became clear that the courts would not sustain the 1989 prohibitions, Congress passed a second law creating the "decency test." The test holds that the NEA, when awarding grants, must "take into consideration general standards of decency and respect for the diverse beliefs and values of the American public."

("Decency" has no precise legal definition and is a subjective judgment, unlike "obscenity," which is illegal in the United States.) The 1990 law also required that grant recipients promise in writing not to violate the "decency" test—a requirement artists quickly dubbed the "loyalty oath." In response, Finley *et al.* extended their suit to challenge the "decency test."

In their case, the artists claimed that the "decency test" discriminates against controversial ideas and that it is vague, thereby casting a shadow over a wide range of art which the NEA will therefore be wary of funding. The artists asked: What precisely is "decency"? What is the line between disagreement and disrespect? Whose "standards," "beliefs," and "values" should artists respect—those of a high school teacher in Brooklyn, a race car driver in Kansas City? Who will determine what these standards are? How can every NEA project reflect the values of all U.S. citizens?

## Creating Ambiguity

In addition to these objections, the artists made a very particular claim about the government's ability to discriminate against ideas in projects that it funds, and it is this part of the case that will most influence artistic, educational, and research institutions. The artists' argument was called "Rust v. Sullivan," a case in which the Supreme Court held that government may indeed select what information is dispensed in federally-funded family planning clinics (to include, for instance, discussion of birth control but to prohibit information on abortion) because government may control (choose, limit) its own speech. Free speech advocates had disagreed, arguing that government money comes from all Americans and that the government may not favor some ideas over others. Though the court rejected this argument in the case of the government's speech, it did rule that government may not discriminate against expression in its programs that support the speech of the people. Since the NEA is such a people's-speech program, the government may not—according to "Rust"—withhold grants on the basis of the content (topic) or viewpoint (pro or con) of grant applicants.

In rejecting the artists' position in Finley *et al.*, the Supreme Court created a middle position between the government's own expression and the people's expression. When the government acts as "patron," the Court said, selecting expression on subjective criteria, the government "may advise" one of its own funding agencies to include "decency" among its standards. The funding agency is then free to follow that advice, or to reject it. "May advise" are the key words for, the Court said, had Congress "required" the NEA to include the "decency test," the requirement would have been unconstitutional. Since Congress only advised the NEA to use the "decency test," it stands. This leaves those seeking government support in an ambiguous position. Since almost all U.S. universities, for example, receive government grants, they, along with artists and research organizations, will be affected by government funding programs that "may" include "decency" as a criteria.

## A Chilling Effect

"In other words," said Marjorie Heins, director of the Arts Censorship project of the American Civil Liberties Union which represented Finley *et al.* against the government, "in this political climate, researchers are less likely to apply to the National Endowment for the Humanities with a proposal that is provocative or highly critical of the government." Such a proposal might be seen as not respecting the "values of the American public" and be refused. "Once a government agency does that, it creates a chilling effect," in which researchers, artists, and writers limit themselves, pursuing less controversial projects in order to get funding. Indeed, the effects of the "decency" clause were quick. According to the National Association of Artists' Organizations, some artists were denied grants, some narrowed the scope of their projects, and others were discouraged from applying altogether (believing their work would be rejected). Moreover, the "decency" clause impeded artists' ability to attract private funding and restricted what artists created with it. Because NEA grants are an imprimatur of excellence, they encourage private backers (in 1993, the $120 million of NEA grants generated $1.1 billion in private support). Failure to get an NEA grant, for whatever reason, reduces an artist's chances of attracting private money.

> *"The 'decency' clause impeded artists' ability to attract private funding and restricted what artists created with it."*

Additionally, should artists find private backing, they are limited in what they may do with it. Since NEA grants are based on artists' past portfolios, any privately-funded work that is not "decent" could impede artists' chances of earning NEA grants in the future.

This chilling has led, wrote columnist Frank Rich in *The New York Times*, to "an increasing wave of self-censorship, in culture both high and low. . . . The more self-censorship that ensues, the more our culture becomes pabulum. Since its Enola Gay disaster [an exhibit about the W.W. II atomic bombing of Japan which veterans groups vehemently protested], the Smithsonian has postponed (apparently forever) an exhibit on the Vietnam War, even as its National Air and Space Museum has staged an elaborate debate-free exhibit on Hollywood's fictional 'Star Wars.'" In the effort to prevent funding controversial work, Congress has required that more NEA grants go to nonurban areas, has prohibited the NEA from awarding grants to individuals (except in literature), and has prohibited institutions that win grants from giving money to third parties. In fact, Heins believes the court's ruling will not significantly affect the NEA because "it is already very cautious. If there isn't political support for funding provocative work, the laws don't matter. The NEA is fighting for its life in Congress. It will be cautious."

> *"Americans have never rested easy with their money going to someone else's project."*

## Suspicious and Puritanical

The debate about public funding for the NEA reflects historical tensions in the American social contract. Suspicious of centralized power, the authors of the Articles of Confederation (1781–1789) gave great government control to localities rather than to the federal government, hobbling counties—much less states—from coordinating economic, civil, and judicial life. The chaos led to the Constitutional Convention and a more binding version of the social contract. Under the Constitution then ratified, citizens contribute (taxes) to a common pool, administered by a central power (state or federal), which pays for projects and polices in their area or other people's areas. Since then, America has been tinkering with the balance of rights between national and state governments, individuals and groups, minorities and majorities. With the unbearable lightness of individualism, Americans have never rested easy with their money going to someone else's project. Those on the Left who withheld taxes during the Vietnam war and those on the Right who have withdrawn into Christian or neo-fascist enclaves and often pay no taxes at all act from the same impulse.

Americans are also a puritanical people, with approach-avoidance feelings about sex. Provocative or sexual imagery thus becomes an "obvious" source for social problems (violence, drugs, unwed mothers, rising welfare rolls). Being pragmatically optimistic, we have a penchant for quick fixes; we believe if we ban the bad pictures, we will be rid of the bad acts. This is the reasoning, for instance, behind the new "family friendly" PAX-TV. As the full-page ad in *The New York Times* informed us, it's "free of explicit sex, free of senseless violence, free of foul language." That'll fix it. Fax me when it's done.

This ban-the-bad-images solution for social problems prevails in spite of large amounts of data, both American and international, experimental and correlational, that pictures of sex (with or without NEA funding) do not cause antisocial conduct. Sadly, neither do pictures of violence, except in the immediate conduct of small children. If you show a three-year-old a video of someone bopping a doll over the head, the child might try bopping his doll. This is not to say the child will become a doll-bopper (or mugger or wife-beater) as an adult. I say "sadly" for if two-dimensional bad images caused bad behavior, we could wipe out the behavior by eliminating the bad pictures. We could promote good conduct by showing good pictures to one and all. This is the optimistic view; it has not yet worked (in controlled experiments, or life). Showing young people movies with "good" values, research has found, does not produce changes in their real-world behavior. Conduct is caused instead by a complex interlocking of three-dimensional factors—biological, familial, social, economic, and political. If a child is raised in a home and community where conflict is addressed by reasonable negotiation most of the time, a steady stream of action movies may prompt some shoot 'em up play acting, but not the world view, values, or identity that motivate lifelong behavior. Changing these complex, real-world motivators is a long, daunting process which offends American can-do-ism. Thus, the NEA found itself the target of two lines of fire—one against federalism and the other against bad pics—both fueled by the great American strengths of optimism, pragmatism, and individualism.

## NEA Supporters and Detractors

In 1965, the NEA was created on the social contract idea of a common pool to support the arts. Grants have ranged from $250,000 for large institutions to $5,000 for individuals. The total NEA budget reached $176 million in 1992, then was trimmed by Congress to $120 million in 1993. The budget for 1999 was $98 million, the result of last-minute concessions by Republicans who did not want to close the agency—as conservatives have been threatening to do since 1995—in an election year since it would offend both wealthy patrons who make tax deductible contributions to the arts and businessmen whose hotels and restaurants benefit from arts-generated tourism. Even when the NEA budget was at its highest, its funds were, as one arts supporter put it, less than the budget for one inch of one B-52 bomber. Grant applications are judged by peer review, rotating panels of artists in the field with particular attention to preventing discrimination against controversial work. As the founding statute says: "Countless times in history, artists and humanists who were vilified by their contemporaries because of their innovations in style or mode of expression have become prophets to a later age." Thus,

> *"The NEA found itself the target of two lines of fire—one against federalism and the other against bad pics."*

the NEA was to "support" and not "control" artistic expression.

Among the achievements of the NEA was the enrichment of the arts in small cities which, without federal support, could not maintain museums or theater, music, and dance programs. Though benefiting millions in this way, the NEA (and state arts councils) became a magnet for public discontent—a Rorschach for the economic anxieties of the Bush recession (Why should I *pay* for art I dislike?) and for the pull between America's individualism and federalism (Why should I pay for art *I* dislike?). NEA detractors have argued that if Americans want art, they'll pay for it at the box office. All other art, they say, is elitist arcana that ordinary folks need not support. NEA supporters have argued that even uncontroversial institutions (such as classical orchestras) cannot survive on ticket sales, and that society has an interest both in supporting new, provocative work and in keeping ticket prices low so that museums, for instance, are democratically accessible.

## Mounting Hostility

The cultural and political climate in which Finley brought her case was marked by mounting hostility to public arts funding. Through the late 1980s and early 1990s, debates had escalated over a number of NEA grants, most famously those to Robert Mapplethorpe, whose photographs include homoerotic nudes and depictions of consensual sadomasochism; artist Andres Serrano, who criticized organized religion by dipping a crucifix in urine; Marlon Riggs, whose expressionistic film *Tongues Untied* accompanies poems (some of them erotic) by African American men; and Artistspace, a gallery whose exhibition catalog criticized the AIDS policies of public officials and the Catholic church. (The Christian, conservative American Family Association (AFA) photocopied each penis pictured in the catalog and sent them to every member of Congress, 3,200 Christian leaders, 1,000 Christian radio stations, 100 Christian TV stations and 178,000 pastors, making the AFA the largest distributor of the offending material.)

> *"NEA supporters have argued that even uncontroversial institutions (such as classical orchestras) cannot survive on ticket sales."*

Though the number of NEA grants that drew complaint was small, right-wing protest against them had two effects. The first was to publicize previously unknown works. When Mapplethorpe's photos were at Cincinnati's Contemporary Arts Center, where both the museum and the exhibit's curator were indicted for obscenity, membership rose 80 percent; over 80,000 people visited the exhibit in seven weeks' time. The second was to build hostility to the NEA as a whole and further the Reagan-era rise in censorship efforts.

According to records kept by The American Library Association, book banning attempts in the United States doubled between 1979–1989. Throughout the 1980s, conservative religious organizations, most prominently the AFA, attacked TV programs and films for discussion of birth control, premarital sex, abortion, homosexuality, and AIDS. Major retail chains dropped "adult" magazines and NC-17 videos (no children under age seventeen permitted) even from special sections where children weren't allowed. Tipper Gore (wife of Vice President Al Gore) founded the Parents Music Resource Center to restrict sales of rock and rap music. The Federal Communications Commission (which regulates broadcast media) sought to expand its ban on controversial programming from the traditional "safe harbor" hours (6 AM–8 PM, when children might be watching) to twenty-four hours per day, limiting all programming to what is suitable for children.

> *"The decency restrictions that Americans may have supported out of a sense of Puritanism . . . may now come back to haunt them."*

With the Finley *et al.* decision, the chilling effects on artists' funding and the development of "controversial" or critical projects *may* now reach the wide range of Americans seeking government funding for their ideas, research, or expression. In other words, the decency restrictions that Americans may have supported out of a sense of Puritanism, pragmatism, and a suspicion of contributing to the common pool may now come back to haunt them as the Court's ruling may allow the government to curtail further the expression of its citizens. Yet the ruling in Finley *et al.* also provides grounds for individuals to sue the government, if they can prove that government "required" a funding agency to reject "indecent" work. This is difficult to prove, as government agencies can always cite lack of artistic merit or simply budget limitations as a reason for refusing a grant. Yet precisely because it is politically advantageous for legislatures in many places in America to announce that they have prohibited the public funding of, say, positive images of homosexuality, or women smeared in chocolate in violation of Finley, they will leave themselves open to such suits. Seeking votes from the political and religious Right, politicians may give artists a new case.

# Serious Arts Cannot Survive Without Government Funding

## by Robert Brustein

**About the author:** *Robert Brustein is a professor of English at Harvard University, the drama critic for the* New Republic *magazine, and the founding director of Yale Repertory and American Repertory Theatres.*

During 1997–1998, the Supreme Court made at least two bad decisions having to do with relations between private behavior and public morality. First, the Court ruled that Paula Jones's civil case could proceed before Clinton left office, on the reasoning that it would not interfere with his conduct of the Presidency—a judicial blunder swiftly exposed by the events of the [subsequent] few months. History will take a bit longer to demonstrate the folly of the Court's eight-to-one decision upholding the decency test in awarding arts grants through the National Endowment for the Arts.

That particular Jesse Helms–sponsored clause, you may remember, commanded the NEA to take into account what it called "general standards of decency and respect for the diverse beliefs and values of the American public" when disbursing money to artists and arts groups. Some concurring justices, believing the 1990 law contained only "advisory language," excused their decision by saying that the clause was essentially "toothless" anyway. Sandra Day O'Connor, for example, declared that the statute would violate the First Amendment if it actually imposed "a penalty on disfavored viewpoints." In other words, you can always appeal to the legal system if you feel your right to speech has been infringed. But if this is so, then why not get rid of the damned thing altogether instead of having to resort to litigation every time the statute is imposed?

Other justices, I believe, read the future more accurately. Disputing O'Connor's sanguine interpretation, Antonin Scalia said that he would consider even an outright ban on federal financing of indecent art to be constitutional.

Clarence Thomas agreed. Only Justice David H. Souter recognized that such a statute, however interpreted or administered, was a form of content restriction, hence a clear instance of viewpoint discrimination, and should have been struck down.

## A Dubious Concept

None of the justices brought up the really vexing question, which is how it ever came to be assumed that the public at large has the right to decide on morality in the arts. The whole notion of "general standards of decency and respect," otherwise known as "community standards," has never been intelligently debated in this country, though this dubious concept has been eloquently denounced by many thinkers, among them Mill, Nietzsche, Ibsen, Shaw, Santayana, Unamuno, and Mencken. It was "community standards" that for years banned works by D.H. Lawrence, Henry Miller, and, most notably, James Joyce, whose *Ulysses* took more than ten years to get published in the United States. In a landmark decision in 1933, John M. Woolsey, a United States District Judge, ruled that while "somewhat emetic, nowhere does [*Ulysses*] tend to be an aphrodisiac." He concluded that the book was therefore not obscene in the legal definition of the word, namely as "tending to stir the sex impulses or lead to sexually impure and lustful thoughts."

So, Americans finally got the chance to ingest the emetic *Ulysses* as a literary supplement to milk of magnesia. But such a definition would have technically prevented us from openly buying erotic books by such authors as Rabelais, Aretino, or Boccaccio, among others more erotic than cathartic. In his classic essay "Pornography and Obscenity," Lawrence ridiculed a British home secretary who harbored a similar definition of obscenity. Outraged over some improper literature, that official had bellowed: "And these two young people, who had been perfectly pure up till that time, after reading this book went out and had sexual intercourse together!!!"—to which Lawrence jubilantly retorted: "One up to them!" Lawrence was hardly a proselytizer for promiscuity. He probably conformed to a stricter moral code than any of his detractors (holding the curious opinion, for example, that masturbation was "the most dangerous sexual vice that society can be afflicted with"). But Lawrence also knew that behind the rabid fulminations of the Comstocks and the Grundys and the Bowdlers lurked a true obscenity, and perhaps the raison d'être of pornography, namely "the grey disease of sex hatred," the desire to keep sex "a dirty little secret." (To him, the emancipated bohemians were not a whole lot better since, in killing off the dirty little secret through public promiscuity and group sex, they also managed to kill off whatever was dark and private in the erotic life.)

> *"How does a community decide an issue of 'obscenity' when no one knows what the term means?"*

188

*Chapter 4*

## The Tyranny of the Majority

Lawrence was even more passionate on the subject of "community standards." First of all, how does a community decide an issue of "obscenity" when no one knows what the term means? Supposedly derived from the Latin *obscena*, meaning that which might not be represented on the stage, it is a word originally driven by the traditional Puritan hostility toward the theater as a form. Since not all of us are Puritans, how then can we arrive at a single community standard? "What is obscene to Tom is not obscene to Lucy or Joe," Lawrence wrote, "and really, the meaning of a word has to wait for majorities to decide it." Majorities, majorities. Only what William Butler Yeats called "the mad intellect of democracy" could ever have devised the caprice that the mass of people corner wisdom in this matter. "We have to leave everything to the majority," Lawrence stormed, "everything to the majority, everything to the mob, the mob, the mob. . . . If the lower ten million doesn't know better than the upper ten men, then there's something wrong with mathematics. Take a vote on it. Show hands, and prove my count. Vox populi, vox Dei [voice of the people, voice of God]."

The talented ten to whom Lawrence alluded have been almost universally scornful of this populist voice of God. Shakespeare had little respect for "the many-headed multitude." John Stuart Mill castigated "the tyranny of the majority." Henrik Ibsen was certain "the majority is always wrong." George Bernard Shaw

> *"Certain crucial needs are not adequately supplied through competition, and chief among these are the serious arts."*

joked that "forty million Frenchmen can't be right." H.L. Mencken inveighed against "boobocracy." In response to which contemporary populists and majoritarians everywhere would undoubtedly unleash their favorite epithet: "elitists."

But like most of the other thinkers, Lawrence had the capacity to distinguish between what he called the "mobself," which mindlessly acquiesces in conventional opinions, and the "individual-self," which is capable of original, subtle, and imaginative thought. People have always longed for an informed electorate. The concept of an enlightened majority has been an elusive ideal ever since the invention of democracy. The most obvious way to achieve this has been through widespread dissemination of works of intellect and the arts. But instead of absorbing the best that has been thought and created in any age, the mass of people in modern industrial societies is invariably bombarded with the most debased forms of opinion and entertainment—being manipulated, diddled, and scammed by those who will use any available means of communication to expand their own powers. It was Lawrence who observed that "the public, which is feeble-minded like an idiot, will never be able to preserve its individual reactions from the tricks of the exploiter." Indeed, the ideal of an enlightened majority grows more and more distant as our advanced technology gets more and more skillful at influencing minds. Today, the religious right, among other influential groups, is using the media to blitz us with all manner of anxieties, hypocrisies, mind gropes, fears, and lies. Americans no longer turn for wisdom to Ralph Waldo Emerson or John Dewey, but to Jerry Falwell and Pat Robertson, if not to Rush Limbaugh, Geraldo, and Don Imus.

The question that remains, however, is federal funding for the arts, and why the public should be required to pay for something that offends the religious or moral sensibilities of some of its members. It is a difficult question to argue without also explaining why the public should pay for something that doesn't interest the great majority—classical music, for example, or modern dance. As John Kenneth Galbraith never tires of reminding us, even in a capitalist society the government is responsible for a number of services not determined by the market—the police department, the fire department, public housing, health, sanitation, education, the courts, government itself. Even a galloping market economy has the capacity to recognize that certain crucial needs are not adequately supplied through competition, and chief among these are the serious arts. Do we need to be told again that the greatest books of any time rarely make the bestseller lists, that the finest works of music are hardly to be found on the pop charts, that the best plays are seldom the biggest box-office bonanzas? Let the market drive the popular arts—Hollywood, Broadway, Madison Avenue, and Motown. The serious arts cannot survive without patronage and support.

> *"I don't see much value in [Robert] Mapplethorpe's X portfolio, but nothing compels me to look at it."*

But what right has government to assess my precious tax dollars if I am not a patron of the opera or a visitor to museums? Put aside the fact that with the present appropriation to the NEA (less than $100 million annually, much of it going to State Arts Councils), I am not even contributing tax dollars, or even a tax dollar, or even half a dollar to the arts, but a figure closer to thirty cents, why should I be required to contribute a penny if there's no immediate benefit?

I don't believe that this is a serious question. If it were, then why wasn't I consulted when being assessed infinitely larger amounts for such inestimable boons to humankind as the Vietnam War, the B-1 bomber, or the Strategic Defense Initiative? It is only when contemplating subsidies to the arts and the humanities that the public is supposed to have a deciding voice. And even then that voice is not respected or heeded: recent polls assure us that most Americans still favor larger Federal subsidies for the arts.

## Not Forced to Look

The nub of the matter remains obscenity and impiety. Should I be obliged to contribute even thirty cents to look at photographs of Robert Mapplethorpe with a whip handle up his butt or be affronted by Andres Serrano's urinedipped crucifix or watch Karen Finley smear her naked body with chocolate syrup? The answer is: I can always turn my face away. One of the blessings of a democracy is freedom of choice. I have the freedom to choose among the countless other works of art available to me, or not to look at anything. The Finley show, the Mapplethorpe photographs and Serrano photographs are only three among thousands of undisputed artworks that have been partially supported by federal subsidy, and no one is requiring me to patronize them.

If I did, however, I might discover that Finley's infamous chocolate act was less designed for prurient display than for making some statement about the female body, just as Andres Serrano's notorious photograph was trying to tell us something about the commercial exploitation of religious objects. I confess I don't see much value in Mapplethorpe's X portfolio, but nothing compels me to look at it. The problem is sectarian sensitivities. In an atmosphere of delicate, easily wounded feelings—an atmosphere to which the politically correct left has certainly contributed a fair share of moans and groans—such expressions were bound to outrage certain factions. Still, it is useful to remember that, in addition to guaranteeing the rights of the majority, our form of government is also dedicated to guaranteeing the rights of dissenting opinion so long as it doesn't incite violence. It is a fact of history that the vanguard has rarely been able to collect a majority

> *"Do Americans wish to be remembered primarily for gangsta rap, Seinfeld, Rent, and Titanic?"*

for its ideas or creations until years after the advances have been absorbed by the establishment.

It is the obligation of a democratic society, however, to protect the magical idea from those who would politicize it into a program or a slogan. And that means, of course, giving support to legitimate visionary artists, no matter how offensive their works may seem to certain organized coalitions. It may not be the primary purpose of the arts to provoke the populace, but this function is often the consequence of any artistic expression attempting to break new ground. American civilization, like all societies, exists not only in the present but in the future as well. We remember Athens less for the Peloponnesian Wars than for Aeschylus, Sophocles, Euripides, Sappho, Plato, and Aristotle. We value the Elizabethans not so much for overcoming the Spanish Armada as for producing the works of Spenser, Marlowe, Shakespeare, and Jonson. We admire Victorian England not for colonizing half the globe, but for bringing forth the novels of Dickens, Thackeray, and George Eliot. Do Americans wish to be remembered primarily for gangsta rap, *Seinfeld*, *Rent*, and *Titanic*? All those attempting to help mold the American future through creative expression, all those who care about how our presentday society will be perceived by posterity, can only be dismayed and appalled by this Supreme Court decision.

# Bibliography

**Books**

| | |
|---|---|
| Richard L. Abel | *Speaking Respect: Respecting Speech*. Chicago: University of Chicago Press, 1998. |
| Richard Delgado and Jean Stefancic | *Must We Defend Nazis? Hate Speech, Pornography, and the New First Amendment*. New York: New York University Press, 1997. |
| Richard Dooling | *Blue Streak: Swearing, Free Speech, and Sexual Harassment*. New York: Random House, 1996. |
| Andrea Dworkin | *Life and Death: Unapologetic Writings on the Continuing War Against Women*. New York: Free Press, 1997. |
| Stanley Eugene Fish | *There's No Such Thing as Free Speech, and It's a Good Thing, Too*. New York: Oxford University Press, 1997. |
| Owen M. Fiss | *The Irony of Free Speech*. Cambridge: Harvard University Press, 1996. |
| Owen M. Fiss | *Liberalism Divided: Freedom of Speech and the Many Uses of State Power*. Boulder, CO: Westview Press, 1996. |
| Henry Louis Gates et al. | *Speaking of Race, Speaking of Sex: Hate Speech, Civil Rights, and Civil Liberties*. New York: New York University Press, 1995. |
| Robert Justin Goldstein | *Burning the Flag: The Great 1989–1990 American Flag Desecration Controversy*. Kent, OH: Kent State University Press, 1996. |
| Kent Greenawalt | *Fighting Words: Individuals, Communities, and Liberties of Speech*. Princeton, NJ: Princeton University Press, 1995. |
| Rochelle Gurstein | *The Repeal of Reticence: A History of America's Cultural and Legal Studies over Free Speech, Obscenity, Sexual Liberation and Modern Art*. New York: Hill and Wang, 1996. |
| Milton Heumann, Thomas W. Church, and David P. Redlawsk, eds. | *Hate Speech on Campus: Cases, Case Studies, and Commentary*. Boston: Northeastern University Press, 1997. |
| Steven J. Heyman, ed. | *Hate Speech and the Constitution*. New York: Garland, 1996. |

# Bibliography

| | |
|---|---|
| Alan Charles Kors | *The Shadow University: The Betrayal of Liberty on America's Campuses*, New York: Free Press, 1998. |
| Garza LaMarche, ed. | *Speech & Equality: Do We Really Have to Choose?* New York: New York University Press, 1996. |
| Laura J. Lederer and Richard Delgado, eds. | *The Price We Pay: The Case Against Racist Speech, Hate Propaganda, and Pornography*. New York: Hill and Wang, 1995. |
| Laurence R. Marcus | *Fighting Words: The Politics of Hateful Speech*. Westport, CT: Praeger, 1996. |
| Wendy McElroy | *XXX: A Woman's Right to Pornography*. New York: St. Martin's Press, 1995. |
| Timothy C. Shiell | *Campus Hate Speech on Trial*. Lawrence: University Press of Kansas, 1998. |
| Nadine Strossen | *Defending Pornography: Free Speech, Sex, and the Fight for Women's Rights*. New York: Scribner, 1995. |
| Samuel Walker | *Hate Speech: The History of an American Controversy*. Lincoln: University of Nebraska Press, 1994. |
| Rita Kirk Whillock and David Slayden, eds. | *Hate Speech*. Thousand Oaks, CA: Sage Publications, 1995. |
| Nicholas Wolfson | *Hate Speech, Sex Speech, Free Speech*. Westport, CT: Praeger, 1997. |
| R. George Wright | *Selling Words: Free Speech in a Commercial Culture*. New York: New York University Press, 1997. |

## Periodicals

| | |
|---|---|
| Floyd Abrams | "Campaign Finance Restrictions Violate the Constitution," *Wall Street Journal*, April 9, 1998. |
| Floyd Abrams | "Look Who's Trashing the First Amendment," *Columbia Journalism Review*, November/December 1997. |
| *American Legion* | Special section on flag desecration Amendment, July 1998. |
| Russ Baker | "The Squeeze," *Columbia Journalism Review*, September/October 1997. |
| Sam Brownback | "The Melodies of Mayhem," *Policy Review*, November/December 1998. |
| Amitai Etzioni | "ACLU Favors Porn over Parents," *Wall Street Journal*, October 14, 1998. |
| Thor L. Halvorssen | "Burning Issues on Campus," *Wall Street Journal*, July 3, 1997. |
| Thomas W. Hazlett and David W. Sosa | "Chilling the Internet? Lessons from FCC Regulation of Radio Broadcasting," *Cato Policy Analysis No. 270*, March 19, 1997. Available from 1000 Massachusetts Ave. NW, Washington, DC 20001. |

193

Charles F. Hinkle          "Can Campaign Finance Reform Coexist with the First
                           Amendment?" *Human Rights*, Winter 1998.

*Issues and*               "Pornography," September 25, 1998.
*Controversies on File*

E. Michael Jones           "What's the Difference Between a Public Library and an X-
                           rated Bookstore?" *Culture Wars*, July/August 1997. Available
                           from 206 Marquette Ave., South Bend, IN 46617.

Wendy Kaminer              "The Rise of 'Respectable' Censorship," *Intellectual
                           Capital.com*, August 14, 1997. On-line. Internet. Available at
                           www.intellectualcapital.com.

Virginia Lam               "Illiberal Arts: Campus Censorship," *World & I*, January
                           1998. Available from 3600 New York Ave. NE, Washington,
                           DC 20002.

Wendy McElroy              "A Feminist Defense of Pornography," *Free Inquiry*, Fall
                           1997.

Barbara Miner              "Reading, Writing, and Censorship," *Rethinking Schools*,
                           Spring 1998. Available from 1001 E. Keefe Ave., Milwaukee,
                           WI 53212.

*Nation*                   "Speech & Power," July 21, 1997.

Charles Oliver             "*The Tin Drum* Meets the Tin Badge," *Reason*, October 1997.

Susan Philips              "Student Journalism," *CQ Researcher*, June 5, 1998. Available
                           from 1414 22nd St. NW, Washington, DC 20037.

Norman Podhoretz           "'Lolita,' My Mother-in-Law, the Marquis de Sade, and Larry
                           Flynt," *Commentary*, April 1997.

Cristopher Rapp            "Chocoholic," *National Review*, July 20, 1998.

David G. Savage            "First Amendment in Your Face," *ABA Journal*, April 1997.

Randall E. Stross          "The Cyber Vice Squad," *U.S. News & World Report*, March
                           17, 1997.

Nadine Strossen            "Regulating Cyberspace," *Vital Speeches of the Day*,
                           December 15, 1997.

Eugene Volokh              "How Free Is Speech When the Government Pays?" *Wall
                           Street Journal*, June 29, 1998.

Jesse Walker               "Rebel Radio," *New Republic*, March 9, 1998.

Shyla Welch                "Should the Internet Be Regulated?" *World & I*, February
                           1998.

Judy Wilkins               "Protecting Our Children from Internet Smut: Moral Duty or
                           Moral Panic?" *Humanist*, September/October 1997.

Elizabeth Wright           "The First Amendment Means Exactly What It Says," *Issues
                           & Views*, Fall 1997. Available from PO Box 467, New York,
                           NY 10025.

Barry Yeoman               "Art & States' Rights," *Nation*, June 29, 1998.

# Organizations to Contact

The editors have compiled the following list of organizations concerned with the issues debated in this book. The descriptions are derived from materials provided by the organizations. All have publications or information available for interested readers. The list was compiled on the date of publication of the present volume; the information provided here may change. Be aware that many organizations take several weeks or longer to respond to inquiries, so allow as much time as possible.

**American Civil Liberties Union (ACLU)**
125 Broad St., 18th Fl., New York, NY 10004-2400
(212) 549-2500
e-mail: aclu@aclu.org • website: http://www.aclu.org

The ACLU is a national organization that defends Americans' civil rights guaranteed in the U.S. Constitution. It adamantly opposes regulation of all forms of speech, including pornography and hate speech. The ACLU offers numerous reports, fact sheets, and policy statements on a wide variety of issues. Publications include the briefing papers "Freedom of Expression," "Hate Speech on Campus," and "Popular Music Under Siege."

**American Library Association (ALA)**
Office for Intellectual Freedom
50 E. Huron St., Chicago, IL 60611
(800) 542-2433
website: http://www.ala.org/oif.html

The ALA is the nation's primary professional organization for librarians. Its Office for Intellectual Freedom (OIF) strives to ensure the public's intellectual freedom as embodied in the organization's Library Bill of Rights, the association's basic policy on free access to libraries and library materials. The OIF monitors and opposes efforts to ban books. It publishes numerous fact sheets and policy statements, including "Protecting the Freedom to Read."

**Cato Institute**
1000 Massachusetts Ave. NW, Washington, DC 20001-5403
(202) 842-0200 • fax: (202) 842-3490
e-mail: cato@cato.org • website: http://www.cato.org

The Cato Institute is a libertarian public policy research foundation. It advocates free-market economics and limited government and strongly opposes regulations on speech. The institute distributes books, policy papers, reports, and the *Cato Journal*, published quarterly.

**Concerned Women for America (CWFA)**
1015 Fifteenth St. NW, Suite 1100, Washington, DC 20005
(202) 488-7000 • fax: (202) 488-0806
website: http://www.cwfa.org

Concerned Women for America is a membership organization that promotes conservative moral values. Its website and monthly magazine *Family Voice* argue against all forms of pornography.

**Electronic Frontier Foundation (EFF)**
1550 Bryant St., Suite 725, San Francisco, CA 94103-4832
(415) 436 9333 • fax: (415) 436-9993
e-mail: ask@eff.org • website: http://www.eff.org

The EEF works to protect privacy and freedom of expression in the arena of computers and the Internet. Its website offers news reports and the *Effector* on-line newsletter. It also publishes the guidebook *Protecting Yourself Online: The Definitive Resource on Safety, Freedom & Privacy in Cyberspace*.

**Freedom Forum**
1101 Wilson Blvd., Arlington, VA 22209
(703) 528-0800 • fax: (703) 284-2836
e-mail: news@freedomforum.org • website: http://www.freedomforum.org

The Freedom Forum is an international organization that works to protect free speech and freedom of the press. It monitors developments in media and First Amendment issues on its website, in its monthly magazine *Forum News*, and in the *Media Studies Journal*, published twice a year.

**Free Speech Coalition**
PO Box 10480, Canoga Park, CA 91309
(800) 845-8503 or (818) 348-9373
e-mail: freespeech@pacificnet.net • website: http://www.freespeechcoalition.com

The coalition is a trade association representing members of the adult entertainment industry. It strives to protect the industry from attempts to censor pornography. The coalition offers fact sheets and other publications about adult entertainment and free speech, including the report *The Truth About the Adult Entertainment Industry*.

**Heritage Foundation**
214 Massachusetts Ave. NE, Washington, DC 20002-4999
(202) 637-9800 • fax: (202) 544-2260
e-mail: pubs@heritage.org • website: http://www.heritage.org

The foundation is a conservative public policy research organization dedicated to free-market principles, individual liberty, and limited government. It favors limiting freedom of the press when that freedom threatens national security. Its resident scholars publish position papers on a wide range of issues through publications such as the weekly *Backgrounder* and the quarterly *Policy Review*.

**Morality in Media (MIM)**
475 Riverside Dr., Suite 239, New York, NY 10115
(212) 870-3222 • fax: (212) 870-2765
e-mail: mimnyc@ix.netcom.com • website: http://www.netcom.com/~mimnyc.

MIM is a national organization that advocates strict enforcement of obscenity standards and opposes indecency in the mainstream media. It adheres to the view that pornography has a harmful effect on society and should be curbed. The organization publishes a newsletter and various articles, research reports, and pamphlets, including the report "Treatment and Healing of Sexual and Pornographic Addictions," the handbook *How to Win the War in Your Community*, and the fact sheet "Cliches About Pornography."

**National Coalition Against Censorship (NCAC)**
275 Seventh Ave., New York, NY 10001
(212) 807-6222 • fax: (212) 807-6245
e-mail: ncac@netcom.com • website: http://www.ncac.org

The coalition represents more than forty national organizations that work to prevent suppression of free speech and the press. It seeks to educate its members and the general public about the dangers of censorship and how to oppose it. NCAC publishes articles, periodic reports, background papers, and the quarterly *Censorship News.*

**National Coalition Against Pornography (N-CAP)**
800 Compton Rd., Suite 9224, Cincinnati, OH 45231-9964
(513) 521-6227 • fax: (513) 521-6337
website: http://www.nationalcoalition.org

N-CAP is an organization of business, religious, and civic leaders who work to eliminate pornography. It encourages citizens to support the enforcement of obscenity laws and to close down pornography outlets in their neighborhoods. Publications include the books *Final Report of the Attorney General's Commission on Pornography*, *The Mind Polluters*, and *Pornography: A Human Tragedy.*

**People for the American Way (PFAW)**
2000 M St., Suite 400, Washington, DC 20036
(202) 467-4999
e-mail: pfaw@pfaw.org • website: http://www.pfaw.org

PFAW works to promote citizen participation in democracy and safeguard the principles of the U.S. Constitution, including the right to free speech. It publishes numerous articles, fact sheets, and position statements on its website and distributes the e-mail newsletter *Freedom to Learn Online.*

# Index

2 Live Crew (rap group), 109
700 Club, 108

ABC-TV, 19, 21
AC/DC (rock group), 108
Academy of American Poets, 173
acid rain, 20
advertising, 38, 39, 70
  American flag in, 66
  and political campaigns on TV, 72–73
*AFA Journal*, 105, 110
Africa, 21–22
African Americans, 12, 13, 64
  influential music created by, 106, 107,
    174–75
  in prison, 89
  and rap music, 78, 88–91, 109
*Age of Innocence* (Hamilton), 25
airline industry, 21
Alabama, 25
Alexander, Jane, 172
Alexander, Lamar, 42, 46
Alien and Sedition Acts of 1798, 97
Alley, Rick, 108
American Arts Alliance, 161, 176
*American Arts Quarterly*, 172
American Association of University
  Professors, 29
American Civil Liberties Union (ACLU),
  23, 69, 81, 82
  on campaign finance, 71, 72
  censorship opposed by, 40, 130, 131, 144
  in the arts, 157, 182
  even at expense of parents' rights, 128
  including Communications Decency
    Act, 122, 125
  website of, 145
American Family Association (AFA), 118,
  123, 143, 185, 186
  and *AFA Journal*, 105, 110
  music lyrics criticized by, 106
American Federation of Labor and
  Congress of Industrial Organizations
  (AFL-CIO), 45

American Library Association (ALA), 101,
  142, 144, 185
  and Banned Book Week, 55, 56, 57
  filtering software opposed by, 113, 131
    because of liberal bias, 125, 127
  has too much power, 81, 82, 128
American Medical Association (AMA), 70
*American Spectator, The*, 53
America Online, 122
Amway Corporation, 71
Angelou, Maya, 23
Aquinas, Thomas, 100
Arizona, 56, 72
arts
  and controversial exhibit on bombing of
    Japan, 162, 183
  government involvement in, is
    inappropriate, 159, 163
  regionalism in, 174
  role of, in society, 160
  supported by many nations, 176
    that differ from U.S., 161
  wide definition of, 166
  *see also* museums; music lyrics; National
    Endowment for the Arts (NEA)
*Austin v. Chamber of Commerce*, 73

Baby Bell phone companies, 71
Bakker, Jim, 21
Baldwin, James, 23
*Baltimore Sun*, 160
Banned Books Online, 145
Banned Book Week, 55, 56, 57
Barnes & Noble, 25
BBC (British Broadcasting Corporation),
  21–22
Beatles, 107
Beeson, Ann, 128
Bennett, William, 137, 153, 155
Best Buy Company, 106
Bible, 106
Black, Hugo, 65
*Black's Law Dictionary*, 115
Blandon, Nelba, 92–93

198

# Index

# Index

# Index